Thinking
About Management

Thinking
About
Management

THEODORE LEVITT

THE FREE PRESS
A Division of Macmillan, Inc.
NEW YORK
Collier Macmillan Canada
TORONTO
Maxwell Macmillan International
NEW YORK   OXFORD   SINGAPORE   SYDNEY

The Free Press
A Division of Macmillan, Inc.
866 Third Avenue, New York, N.Y. 10022

Collier Macmillan Canada, Inc.
1200 Eglinton Avenue East
Suite 200
Don Mills, Ontario M3C 3N1

Printed in the United States of America

printing number

3 4 5 6 7 8 9 10

Library of Congress Cataloging-in-Publication Data

Levitt, Theodore
    Thinking about management/Theodore Levitt.
        p.   cm.
    Includes index.
    ISBN 0-68-486399-5
        1. Management.   2. Organizational change.   I. Title.
HD31.L3848   1991   90–43894
658—dc20   CIP

Credits and Acknowledgments

Grateful acknowledgment is made to the publishers who have granted permission to reprint the following selections:

"The Thinking Manager" was adapted with permission from *Health Management Quarterly* (Second Quarter 1990), p. 6, a publication of The Baxter Foundation.

These articles are reprinted by permission of *Harvard Business Review* and copyrighted by the President and Fellows of Harvard College; all rights reserved: "Management and Knowledge" (May/June 1989), p. 8, © 1989; "Decisions" (January/February 1989), p. 6, © 1989; "Command and Consent" (July/August 1988), p. 5, © 1988; "The Mixed Metrics of Greed" (November/December 1987), pp. 6–7, © 1987; "Rascality and Virtue" (March/April 1987), p. 4, © 1987; "Convictions" (July/August 1989), p. 8, © 1989; "Betterness" (November/December 1988), p. 9, © 1988; "Innovation" (November/December 1989), p. 8, © 1989; "The Youthification of Management" (September/October 1987), p. 4, © 1987; "The Innovating Organization" (January/February 1988), p. 7, © 1988; "On Agility and Stability" (March/April 1988), p. 7, © 1988; "Fast History" (March/April 1989), p. 8, © 1989; "Deliriums of Entrepreneurship" (originally published as "The LSD of the 1980s") (May/June 1987), p. 4, © 1987; "Entrepreneuring Eastern

Contents

To the Reader   ix

PART ONE   THINKING

1. The Thinking Manager   3
2. The Not-Good Manager   11
3. Management and Knowledge   16
4. Management Talent and Knowledge Work   20
5. Decisions   25
6. Command and Consent   29
7. The Mixed Metrics of Greed   33
8. Rascality and Virtue   39
9. Convictions   42

PART TWO   CHANGING

10. Betterness   51
11. Innovation   55
12. The Youthification of Management   58
13. The Innovating Organization   64
14. On Agility and Stability   67

CONTENTS

15. Fast History   70
16. Deliriums of Entrepreneurship   73
17. Entrepreneuring Eastern Europe   77
18. Futurism and Management   81

    PART THREE   OPERATING

19. The Chryslerization of America   99
20. The Pluralization of Consumption   103
21. Customers, Money, and Conscience   109
22. Making Sense About Strategy and Customers   112
23. Business-to-Business Business   116
24. Cost Evasions and Gross Margin Escapes   124
25. The Marketing Mode   131
26. Trust in Advertising   138
27. The Law of the Lunch   146

    Index   149

To the Reader

THE EFFECTIVE MANAGER does lots of things, but there are at least three things he or she must do: think about the purposes of the organization and the directions in which it must be led; foster and manage change; and conduct operations so that the organization and its people function effectively and efficiently. The briefings in this book are therefore divided into three sections: Thinking, Changing, Operating.

If there is one thing that most characterizes the effective manager, it is the fusion of decisiveness and ability to act, regardless of circumstance and uncertainty. It is not generally supposed that this ability also has anything to do with cerebration, with thinking. But of course it does. One doesn't have to be a visibly agonizing thinker to think about what one concludes and what one does. Indeed, precisely because managers are decisive and action oriented, they are seldom recognized for the thinking that precedes the actions they take.

In this book's section called "Thinking," the thinking that the effective manager must do is explicitly spoken about, and, on various matters, actually provided. One hopes that the economy and simple clarity with which the book tries to do this will not detract from its being taken seriously or cause pain or regret when it is.

"Changing" is another section of the book. Much confusion attends the matter of change, and often some very wrong-headed actions. The more strongly people believe they are bombarded and burdened by change, the more likely they are simply to react to it and the less likely to think about it. Though recent years have been characterized by certain dramatic changes, there is much less certifiable change than appears. Much is merely activity, brief spasms or eruptions that return soon to relative quiescence. It is useful to distinguish between activity and change, and to focus also on what does not change, what is firm and abiding, and especially to note the central continuing tendencies of society and business.

Of course, there is much change—which can also be said of other periods in modern times. The Industrial Revolution was, after all, called a "revolution," though not, it may be noted, during its time. That we refer to our times as revolutionary is not entirely a presumption. It refers to the ubiquity and intensity of the accelerations to which we are subjected, and which we ourselves create.

Creating and managing change is the central activity of management. Managers make decisions. Decisions deal with choices. Choices involve alternatives, which include possibilities for making, avoiding, resisting, and creating change. Where there are not possibilities of change there is no need for managers. Administrators will do, and so also their lower levels of compensation. Effective managers need to be smart, informed, and judicious. They should also have courage and conviction, and these are also treated in the section "Changing."

Regarding the subjects grouped under the section "Operating," the one on "The Pluralization of Consumption" is perhaps indicative. It argues that in all product categories, global competition is now increasingly characterized by the presence and growth of multiplying numbers of market segments; that these segments now appear everywhere in the developed parts of the world, and even increasingly in underdeveloped or developing parts. Many of these segments, especially in gastronomy, entertainments, and personal adornments (the so-called "high-touch" sectors of life), have certain ethnic origins and identities that now travel and prevail globally. The operating demands these make on modern management in our increasingly globalized commercial society are new, challenging, not widely understood, and capable of causing both exhilaration and exhaustion.

The briefings in this book are themselves designed to be anything but exhausting—rather, they are brief and intended to be facilitating. If they don't help the reader think and function more effectively, something is wrong, either with what I've done or what I've assumed. Whatever may be wrong, it is entirely my doing, though one hopes not anybody's undoing.

Helping me in all this has been my assistant and friend, Georgette Dikmak, to whom I am grateful.

THEODORE LEVITT
Harvard Business School
1990

ONE

Thinking

1

The Thinking Manager

FEW THINGS ARE more important for a manager to do than ask simple questions: why do we do it; why that way; what are the alternatives; how much does it cost; why are costs up; who does it cheaper and better; what's happening out there that's likely to hurt or help us? It is not to get answers that the good manager asks these and other questions, but to get people to think rather than just to act, react, or administer.

A newly installed chief financial officer asked, "How many warehouses and distribution centers do we have? How many did we have five years ago?" There had been no change. Given that everything else had changed—a shift from rail transport to more flexible, vastly improved highway systems with bigger and faster trucks, he asked, "With what minimal number of warehouses could we now satisfy our retailers? What would that cost?"

The questions led to a massive mathematical model of the system. Sure enough, the optimal number of warehouses was revealed to be much below the present. He then asked more questions: "Instead of just reducing the number, what would happen if we started over from scratch? What would be the optimal combination of optimally sized, optimally technologized warehouses using the best possible computerized communications links with our customers?"

Before it was all over, warehouses had been entirely eliminated in favor of a small handful of huge and highly automated distribution centers, with 24-hour-a-day computerized communications with all customers. In time, costs fell steeply while service levels and market shares rose.

Most managers manage for yesterday's conditions, because yesterday is where they got their experiences and had their successes. But management is about tomorrow, not yesterday. Tomorrow concerns what should be done, not what has been done. "Should" is determined by the external environment—what competitors (old, new, and potential) can and might do, the choices this will give customers and those who advise or direct customers, the rules constantly being made by governments and other players, demographic changes, advances in generalized knowledge and technology, changing ecology and public sentiments, and the like.

Consider demographics. Having learned how to manage in an age of labor abundance and widespread English-language literacy, we are not exactly best prepared for

4

managing in other times that may be approaching or are already upon us. Negative incentives (the threat of getting punished or fired) may no longer work so reliably, and, in any case, it would be more costly to fire and then hire new people than to train the people we have and shift to positive incentives.

Or consider technology and the inventory problem. With bar codes on most packages, with low-cost, easy-to-operate personal computers throughout most organizations, and with rapid overnight delivery from distant places, there is no longer any need to keep large stocks of supplies in inventory. It's easy to know exactly what's moving out of inventory and when to reorder. And with high capital costs (the cost of carrying inventory), the incentive is especially strong to keep stocks low; not just stocks in a central location but in all the offices, labs, and workplaces where they are used. For all of us a simple visual inspection often reveals excesses of almost all supplies. Nor does it require an expert to make that determination. When my son broke a finger in a hockey game, I went with him to the hospital emergency room to which he'd been assigned to wait. I looked at the open cupboards. There must have been three dozen of every variety and shape of metal splints, cases of Betadine in varying volumes, huge quantities of individually packaged cotton, and the like. All I could think of was a major conflagration—was that what all this was for? Why else this abundance?

The experience raised my consciousness, and, to my horror, for the first time I saw the same excesses in my secretary's office—enough pencils, paper clips, file folders, pads, typewriter ribbons, and the like to last way past retirement. Why?

5

To be a model modern manager supposes a very good management information system. Great masses of data get disgorged in impressive magnitudes, or can be called up for instantaneous revelation on your PC. But why don't things seem to get managed better as a consequence? Why do you feel so swamped and harassed?

Data are not information. Information is not meaning. Just as data require processing to become informational, so information requires processing to become meaningful.

Yet the more abundant the information, the less meaning it seems to yield. All seems, instead, congestion and confusion. The surest way to destroy a person's capacity for discrimination and good judgment is to bombard him or her with an enormous abundance of data, even if it's incontestably relevant. The greater the variety of good food consumed at a meal, the less you appreciate each dish. The louder the noise, the less clear the message.

What is needed is discrimination in the supply and use of data, not their sheer abundance, regardless of relevance. Discrimination cannot be exercised in a vacuum. Magnitudes must be limited to what is relevant and comfortably usable. The effective use of information is governed by the principle of parsimony: limit it to the more-or-less precise purpose at hand. A good thing is not necessarily improved by its multiplication. The governing question is: what is the question to be answered, the problem to be illuminated, the matter to be explored, the issue to be defined? And it is precisely because these are not self-defining concepts that it is essential to think them through in advance, because no amount of data will tell you what information you'll need to get at the right questions.

The Irish Tourist Board was enormously pleased with data that showed the success of its promotional efforts. And exit questionnaires showed that exactly the targeted people (well-off big spenders) were coming to Ireland. But the relevant data were not how many visitors had come and how much they'd spent. It turned out that the high-spending tourists stayed mostly in foreign-owned urban hotels, drank imported Scotch whiskey, ate imported beefsteak, and rented imported cars. Upon reflection, what was wanted was spending on what Ireland uniquely produced. What was therefore wanted was tourists satisfied, perhaps even especially pleased, to stay in less luxurious domestically owned hotels or bed-and-breakfasts, eating indigenous food in modest local restaurants, drinking Irish beer and Irish whiskey in small-town Irish pubs, taking trains and buses, stretching their money by having picnic lunches of local foods bought in small-town stores. Data showing fewer, perhaps less affluent and more parsimonious visitors would have been better.

The faster and more acrobatically the computer can perform, the greater the necessity that its presumed beneficiaries must first think about what it's all for.

Unfortunately, thinking is not much in vogue. Experience is what mostly counts in selecting people for management positions—preferably successful experience. This is powerfully attested by the authority accorded to people in meetings who "talk from experience," and by the opprobrium implied in the observation "That may be all right in theory, but . . ." Theory, like thinking, is held in low relative esteem. To think your way through to a solution is to imply absence of recourse to the important thing that really counts—experience.

7

Where careful thought *is* acknowledged as a prerequisite for effective executive action, this capability is so widely presumed to be inappropriate for a line executive that a separate organizational entity has been created especially for it. This entity is called "staff." And wherever one sees an expansion of the staff one also sees its widening isolation from decision-making authority.

Yet the isolation is more structural than real. The more difficult and bigger the decision, the more likely that the staff, or some outside consultants or advisors, are called to take a hand. Increasingly, managers withhold complex decisions until "all the facts are in" and the situation has been "thoroughly studied." Judgment is suspended until the staff has reported.

But finally when the decision comes, it is neither a decision nor a judgment that's being made. It is only a choice—and generally not even a choice between alternatives. Rather, the choice is only between accepting or rejecting the staff's heavily documented recommendations. Seldom is there a choice as between two or more positive alternatives. What passes for thinking among those who must decide tends to be little more than rambling committee discussions of the ins and outs of issues carefully predigested, documented, resolved, and set forth by the staff. Seldom is there a quiet moment for independent contemplation by the deciders themselves.

This is far different from less sophisticated times, when limited and less "processed" data put a heavy burden on the manager to synthesize the meager facts that were available and to think things through, relying heavily on experience, intelligence, wit, wisdom, animal energy, and daring. The result in the past may often have been awful, but perhaps not without consequent benefit—because it is not from experience that we learn the most, but from bad experience.

Not that this kind of seat-of-the-pants decision-making is to be preferred. Far from it. But it is helpful for managers to see the difference between then and now, to see exactly what happens as they ascend in organizational position. Most likely as they rise they get ever more staff help for important decisions. This is both comforting and addictive. Less and less needs be done for oneself, including thinking. Everyone will deny that such negligence applies personally, of course. Nevertheless there is more time for visible, active, involving, and commendable activities. One circulates. One talks to and encourages others. One manages by walking around—provided, of course, that's not the only way.

Unfortunately, something gives. As with any other skill or art, disuse produces disability. Those who, by virtue of their position, rely increasingly on their staffs to do their analyses and thinking for them are increasingly incapacitated to do precisely what is so vital at increasingly higher ranks—to think seriously and deeply for themselves about the purposes of the organizations they head or functions they perform, about the strategies, tactics, technologies, systems, and people necessary to attain these purposes, and about the important questions that need always to be asked.

The most precious thing a manager brings to a job is the wisdom conferred by experience—precisely so that he or she can operate decisively and effectively with limited information, with dispatch and confidence. But when change accelerates, when it comes unexpectedly from constantly unexpected directions, when new technologies and social and environmental conditions occur so disjunctively, the wisdom conferred by experience needs help. That is one reason professional staffs and consultants proliferate. It is also a reason why now, in this unaccustomed age of rapid acceleration, this hazardous new age of fast history, that managers must also take time to think carefully for themselves, because, in the metaphorical cadence of Robert Graves,

> Experts ranked in serried rows
> Filled the enormous plaza full.
> But only one is there who knows
> And he's the man who fights the bull.

2

The Not-Good Manager

GOOD MANAGERS HAVE strong colleagues. Those that don't are not good. In a very short time it will show.

Good managers either inherit good managers or hire good ones to replace the not-good ones. If they don't replace not-good managers, they themselves are not good.

Good managers are self-assured, clear-minded, clear-spoken, and decisive, and they keep things simple. They are actively dissatisfied with poor performers and will not long delay in replacing them. Unfortunately, not-good managers also replace their own well-performing managers, though usually less quickly. But they cannot tolerate strong and accomplishing colleagues. Strong and accomplishing colleagues make weak bosses uncomfortable. They are irritants and threats, however useful they otherwise are. Reasons and ways will be found to push them out. Furthermore, good managers will not long tolerate working with or for not-good managers. They get out. What is finally left organizationally is the residuum—the bottom of the process of downward natural selection.

Symptoms of the not-good manager are more varied than those of the good manager. A not-good manager can be pleasant and likeable or unpleasant and abrasive, but is more likely to be outwardly patient and indulgent than to have a short or explosive temper.

Nor is this to say that a good manager is naturally and obviously talented, or that you can tell talent by results. Results are conditioned by numerous externals, the most common consequence of which is for good times to be mistaken for good management. But a careful look at the relative performance of companies in an industry usually reveals chronic underperformers, and they will underperform by almost all applicable standards.

Much blame for bad performance is put on suddenly bad or changing times, and on severe and unfair, preferably foreign, competitors. But since it is management's job to manage for right results, regardless of circumstance, no such excuses can be warranted.

The general rule may be laid down that bad performance reflects the existence of bad management. That is especially so in the case of bad relative performance that remains relatively bad for two years or more.

Some problems are, of course, intractable. In such cases, the only solution is abandonment. Failure to abandon is itself a failure of management: management has not seen or understood the facts that face it, and has not faced them

12

with prompt and decisive action. Nor is Moshe Dayan's verbal maneuver an excuse, however convenient. When asked about the problem of the West Bank, he said, "A problem is something with a solution. If there is no solution, there is no problem." Abandonment *is* a solution, however inconvenient.

Not-good managers are generally very good at explaining how much better things are than they seem, and what bunch of things are being or will be done to make them even better. That in part explains their tenure, why they exhaust and outlast critics on their boards and in the financial community. They sound better than they are.

It is obvious to the rankest amateur why strong associates and strong subordinates are so important. It is in their domains that most of the work that needs doing is done. Only a little of the work of a business gets done at the top, however important that work is. The rest gets done where the real work actually is, which is "below" and "out there." If it does not get done there, or get done well, not even the best corporate strategies, the best information systems, the best organizational structure or routines, or the best corporate citizenship will help. Looking at the scattered parts of the clock he'd tried madly to fix, the frustrated Hatter cried to Alice, "And I used the *best* butter, the *best,* and it still doesn't work." Real work requires effective efforts.

In an actively competitive world, ineffectualness soon shows up on the bottom line. It is not enough that right actions are taken. They must also be timely and vigorous. Right measures confidently taken produce contagious confidence and energy. These are at least as necessary for the effective execution as competence itself.

13

When heads of companies or departments chronically exhibit self-doubt or irresolution in the face of troubles and pressures, or equivocate constantly about changes that must be faced or opportunities that arise, everything declines. Mediocrity festers and proliferates because strong and decisive colleagues will not have stayed around. Company performance will turn and stay bad, no matter how good the times or seemingly good the performance.

Not all competitors perform equally well during good times. It is well to know where one stands relative to them. There is always a way to measure how well or badly a company, a division, or a department is doing. There are absolute or relative measures of market share, return on managed assets, inflation-adjusted productivity per employee, and cash flow, as well as others, of course. Usually it is sensible to look at two or more in tandem. Never is it acceptable to look with satisfaction at absolute numbers alone, or with absolution at reverses also suffered by competitors.

We decline in energy as we advance in age; also in decisiveness and daring. All people finally wear out. Companies with strong and confident managements increasingly find humane ways of reassigning or letting declining people go. At the top they have the self-assurance to do what must be done and the strength to find acceptable ways.

Some very effective companies use less humane ways. They operate according to harsh Spencerian principles. Each year some prescribed minimum percent of managers are required to be let go, starting qualitatively "at the bottom," without regard to management level. Heads of large divisions, and in at least one known case the president himself, have gotten the axe. The strength and quality of the surviving cadre ratchets ever upward over the years, until the organization becomes "all muscle."

"All muscle" is not an acceptable life for everyone, nor even verifiably necessary for outstanding performance. Nor is it a sufficient principle to justify the removal of weak managers. But what is absolutely intolerable, and for which no justification is possible, is an organization whose boss is almost totally ringed with weak and therefore chronic underperformers. In the end the price for everybody will be too high. First there will be gradual decay of competitiveness, relative decline in all the critical numbers, then absolute decline, and finally the annihilation of assets, jobs, and general well-being.

It can be said with confident certainty that wherever the articulate and persuasive rationalizer for constantly or frequently poor performance regularly shows up, the company will surely slow down and go under.

3

Management and Knowledge

BABE RUTH KNEW a lot about hitting homers. The fact that he didn't know exactly what he knew, and couldn't explain it, didn't keep him from hitting homers. When he tried to explain, nobody got it, and he fell into a slump. Try that on yourself—explaining in a few paragraphs what you know and what makes you successful.

You do not need to know what you know in order to use it and use it very well. Like Ruth, in order to use it, you don't have to be able to explain it. Yet if you don't know what makes what you do work, it is awfully hard to repeat, multiply, or improve on, and that can cause big problems when you're trying to fix what's gone wrong. That is why

16

good companies institutionalize, routinize, and document what they do and how they operate, why they regularly examine themselves with a self-critical eye.

Knowledge is peculiar. It has the special quality of enriching those who receive it without impoverishing or diminishing those who give it away. But the most precious of all knowledge can be neither taught nor otherwise passed on.

This helps explain why the practice of management has not noticeably improved these past decades in line with the enormous effluence of business texts and how-to books, business magazines, courses, and ghosted autobiographies of celebrity practitioners.

Not everything that can be learned can be taught. Not everything that's learned is done so consciously. A young child screams with pain upon touching a hot stove. A little loving comfort and mild medication soon make things well, except for a small blister. That evening the parent, returning home, greets the child as usual: "Hi—and what did you learn today?" "Nothing," comes the cheerful response. But never again will the child touch the burner, except cautiously, even when the stove is cold.

Some knowledge is subconscious, so deeply embedded that it seems instinctive or, as is often said, "a God-given talent," like Mozart's or great managers'. Because possessors of that kind of knowledge are not even dimly aware of what they know and have, they cannot effectively explain, teach, or talk about it, even though they can lead others to do what must be done. Their secret is the talent that they implement. What gets told and explained are merely stories, beliefs, protocols, advice, and tricks of the trade, but not authentic knowledge, wisdom, or talent. The

17

latter qualities are special. They are existential—traits, characteristics, or conditions that are developed mysteriously over time and shaped by experience. And usually the process begins early, as in early childhood. They do not easily travel via books or lectures, like arithmetic or particle physics. Mostly they travel only with their possessors.

Knowledge is valued for its utility, which is why we institutionalize education. The paradox is that the less teachable something is, the rarer and therefore more valuable it is. The most important things the general manager knows and does involve that kind of knowledge—inherent, authentic, and resistant to teachability but not to learnability. That explains why really outstanding managers tend to emerge gradually from the pack, and occasionally suddenly in special circumstances, rather than being specifically selected or trained for command. Selection and training are mostly filtering devices for finding people with a largely inexplicable mix of promising characteristics and revealed talents. These devices should not pass unappreciated, but neither should they be mistaken for the real things they try to identify.

The more talk there is these days about "the age of the knowledge worker," the more rubbish gets talked about it. The most important thing for the manager to know about knowledge is not that some kinds can be taught and others cannot, but that the more professionalized and valued either gets, the less its possessor is dependent on an employer for its use and for his or her employment.

That explains the increasing mobility of professional managers who move from one employer to another. Like other professionals (as in law, electrical engineering, information systems, finance, manufacturing) their bonds and loyalties must be stronger to their professions than to their employers. They can leave their employers but keep their professions.

The more dependent the work of an organization is on the work of its professional knowledge workers (which include its managers), the more the organization must attend to their getting the professional and personal satisfactions that keep them inspired and in place. Whether they will depart to other places is only partly a matter of demand on the outside. Whether and how well they will perform is almost entirely a matter of conditions in the inside.

Two great challenges lie increasingly ahead for the modern organization: to have the requisite types and numbers of knowledge workers to do what must be done, and to have an organization in which they will thrive and with which they will want to remain.

4

Management Talent and Knowledge Work

THE DIFFERENCE BETWEEN line work and staff work is real, but not any longer really relevant.

Much of what used to be distinguished as being staff work was held in limited esteem; meaning not so much low esteem as that high esteem was reserved for those who did what was considered the real work of the organization.

The distinction between line and staff work gets blurred and less important as the work of what might now be called staff work gets more important. In any case, lots of people principally engaged in staff activities are managers, which is one of the chief characteristics of line work, regardless how distant it may be from the much celebrated firing line.

20

And "firing line" is a fitting metaphor, the concept of line and staff having been invented by the military, where, in the olden days, the difference between being in the line or at headquarters could be a matter of life and death.

"Staff work" has gotten more important as the nature, sources, and pace of competition have changed. As with warfare, these changes have been driven by technology. In warfare, when the enemy's position, numbers, armaments, and movements can no longer be directly observed on what used to be a fixed field of battle, they have to be inferred. That leads to the establishment of organized systems for gathering and analyzing intelligence. The skills and training required for that kind of work are not the same as those of soldiers at the front. The staff that is required is a new professional breed, no longer consisting only of experienced and wise adjutants, and orderlies to cook and fetch. All this is also true of business.

The technologies that change the enemy also change your own forces. They no longer stretch out visibly before you for relatively easy observation and direction. New communications, reporting, and control systems get installed, as do new kinds of staff professionals. It is impossible for the line to function without them.

It is understandable that the staff professionals who supply line commanders with data, analyses, and status reports be also asked to make recommendations, that their counsel be routinely sought regarding strategy and tactics, with respect to which decision-making and accountability for results remain uniquely the responsibilities of line management.

It is also understandable that some staff professionals, though totally lacking in line experience, will be spotted for

21

their managerial possibilities and be appointed directly to important and even high-level line jobs. Sometimes their line-management capabilities will have already been clearly demonstrated; sometimes they are simply being tested, tried out to see directly what they can do.

In important decisions regarding appointments to important management jobs, the old presumptions of staff/ line differences recede. Special merit and confidence still attach to line experience. But there are new facts. Specialized knowledge and knowledge work become increasingly important and proportionally greater in the work of business. As the proportion of knowledge workers expands, increasingly managers will have to come from the knowledge cadre. And increasingly it helps for managers themselves to possess specialized knowledge.

The specialized knowledge of the knowledge worker is learned knowledge. It is therefore reasonable to presume that managerial capability is also learnable, like algebra. But knowing algebra does not a mathematician make. Nor does learning to read music or play the violin make a professional performer. First, there must be sufficient, and the right kind of, talent. It is a firmly established fact that this cannot be learned. So also of management ability.

A person's managerial possibilities reside largely in personal qualities and intelligences—in talents that are largely inherent or at least were acquired and developed in early childhood. Management capability is not the same as management talent. Both can be improved by experience and schooling. Talent itself cannot in these ways be acquired, but it can be spotted. In a world of increasing and specialized knowledge, schooling becomes a requisite and a facilitator. It is increasingly essential for admission to opportunities to be spotted for possession of managerial possibilities.

Management ability is not a matter of IQ-type intelligence, although there is a reasonable presumption that IQ intelligence is a requisite for some of the specialized knowledge or calculation that management work entails. But in no demonstrable ways are high IQ scores or superior school performance predictors of, or even correlates of, managerial success.

Timing and happenstance have a great deal to do with success in the world of affairs, particularly the success that is measured by position in the large complex organization. When success is measured by personal wealth, much has to do with circumstance, such as of family and other connections. Nor is success in management much a matter of being especially visionary, insightful, or prophetic. Yet these are important and can be decisive, provided the individual in the first place has the energy and kinds of special personal qualities that generate confidence and engage the convictions and efforts of the people he or she needs to do the work that needs doing.

If managerial talent does not correlate with IQ scores or superior school performance, and if it cannot be learned but only cultivated and extended, then, organizationally speaking, a special premium attaches to its discovery, and especially early in life, lest the advantages of youthful vigor and energy be long foregone. It is therefore one of the most important tasks of the mature and experienced manager to be constantly attentive to the discovery of younger people who emanate signals, however weakly, of managerial potential.

23

It is not necessary that the observer be able to describe or articulate the signs of managerial potential. It is enough that the observer somehow feels that a particular person has special talents or attributes. That should be enough, because it is precisely in a person's emanations that his or her managerial talents lie. There is relatively little risk in putting those emanations to work. In any case, for younger people there are lots of relatively low-risk managerial jobs into which they can be placed for progressive and tolerant testing, where they can be observed and coached long enough to see tangibly if something is really there.

5

Decisions

IN MOST BUSINESS SITUATIONS, decisions just happen. They are seldom made affirmatively or decisively. Mostly they emerge gradually—from analyses, observations, comparisons, discussions, and the passage of time. Decisions made with confident rationality and swiftness occur mostly in the manufactured constructions of braggarts out for instant plaudits.

Brisk decisiveness without the benefit of deep knowledge or experience is rare. Mostly it occurs in frustration, anger, or rage, and with commensurate consequences. Its incidence is widely exaggerated, and so are its successes.

The world of managerial work and responsible decision-making does not work according to the representations of journalists in need of breezy copy, or according to the muscular or visionary ways of ghosted autobiographies, and certainly not according to the prescriptions of sweaty inspirationalists on the speaking circuit.

Successful work requires real work. It doesn't get done with rhetoric, wishfulness, or shortcuts. It requires discipline and good sense, and thoroughness proportionate to what is known and what is at stake. It should be free of laboriousness and pretension and be driven by an urge to get on with things rather than dawdle and delay. More work is not necessarily better work, and obsessively bureaucratic work is definitionally bad work. But not all bureaucratic work is bad.

The organization exists to regularize results. It marshals resources for predictable outcomes. It requires discipline, order, and control as well as people who willingly submit to these strictures, who will reliably do what is prescribed day in and day out. Bureaucracy, prescription, and routine are not just consequential; they are necessary and therefore inherent. They are also deadening. But because they are necessary for the organization to do what it exists to do, some opposing other things must also be done to keep the organization alive and creative.

Some of those other things can be institutionalized, as is the case with research and development, organized analysis of competition and markets, and long-range planning. But some cannot. Without visionaries, inspirators, and muscular movers, much of the world's new and better work would not get done. They originate new enterprises and new ways. And they are especially needed in the larger and more complex organization, where routine and bureaucracy are likely to be most rigidly embedded. One can hardly do too much to cultivate and encourage such people inside the modern organization.

Yet more is not necessarily better. A symphony orchestra, consisting characteristically of individualists of great individual talents, works only because its disciplined performers submit to somebody else's tune. So also soccer, hockey, basketball, and other team sports: every effectively functioning organization is a disciplined organization of willing team players, no matter how energetic or innovative each player is capable of being.

The entrepreneurship of each participant is most useful when harnessed to the organization's purposes and capabilities, provided that the organization also has people who have the vision to transcend the ordinary and the muscle to drive the pace—and who will inspire others with talent and inclination to go beyond the routines for which the organization exists.

"An army of rabbits commanded by a lion is better than an army of lions commanded by a rabbit," said Napoleon. No wonder Thomas Carlyle said Napoleon had words in him like Austerlitz battles. Yet Napoleon is better known for his deeds than for his words. His deeds belonged to opposing genres—the deeds of the imaginative strategist and daring commander who inspired commitment, energy, action, and innovation; and the deeds of the practical operator who installed rigid codes of governance and fixed routines that remain to this day models for superbly functioning organizations throughout the world. These opposing types of deeds reciprocated and complemented one another. The latter enabled the former, and the former guided the latter. From this kind of well-ordered context

27

and complexity one gets decisions that are rational and reliable, as well as daring and courageous.

Nothing is simple or one-dimensional. But neither is anything so complex that it cannot profit from the sensibility of common sense or the muscularity of prophetic vision.

In the end, victory comes to those who attack each task with the passion of the scientist and the precision of the artist.

6

Command and Consent

THE HISTORY OF great management and leadership accomplishments is always the history of an individual's special qualities. Prime Minister Churchill did not rally Britain by showing the people pie charts, opinion surveys, or grids of competitive analysis.

What's true of nations is also true of businesses.

A person may be appointed to high position, but never to leadership. Leaders are effective via the authority conferred on them by those on whom they depend for results. This requires evidence that the leader's vision, purposes, and convictions are based on solid contact with the grit and grind of things as they really are.

The manager who knows the world mostly through the refractions of completed staff work, and acts only after

receiving elaborate studies whose conclusions and prescriptions have been squeezed into organizational consensus, does not lead.

Nobody gets inspired or energized by those who govern
only by the consensual numbers, who draw generalized
conclusions but have no independent convictions.

Leaders produce consent, others seek consensus. Consent is given to the confident and composed, those with
firm and persuasive convictions. Only people who believe
in themselves generate believers. Nor is it a matter of
charisma. It is about inner strength and clearly articulated
views that are convincingly based on deep experience and
solid judgments. Arrogance and swagger sometimes work,
but then things fall apart.

In the big professionally managed organization, things
are held together by accepted routines and rational decision-making. Yet too many managers too often depend too
heavily on too much staff work before doing their own
work. Higher rank distances them from direct contact with
where the daily action is.

In high positions, they develop an almost obligatory
tendency to do the opposite of what formerly got them
promoted ever higher. Below they acted with the easy
decisiveness that came from direct contact with what was
being acted upon. Now higher up, they act with the tedious
deliberativeness that accompanies dependence on second-
ary sources of information.

Things are different in fast-moving new companies and
in fast-moving fields such as retailing, where top managers
constantly "walk the stores" and "talk" their competitors'
merchandise. Distance and absence of direct contact with

everyday reality lead to irresolution, mistakes, and quick calamity.

Because high position in the large organization extends the manager's reach, there is more at stake, and so it is presumed that prudence requires big decisions to be deeply researched and carefully calculated. That may be right, but it is no substitute for earthy contact with the way things actually are.

It is precisely the large organization's deeply embedded routines and relationships, its inherent inertia and obedience to Newton's first law (the one about a body at rest remaining at rest), that reduces the risks normally associated with brisk managerial decisiveness. The large organization, like the elephant, is relatively immovable, certainly not easily pushed over or around. It can usually weather bad decisions precisely because almost nothing can happen very fast—either in it or to it. Midcourse corrections are possible because things move slowly. And the cost of false moves will usually be small compared to what remains unmoved and intact. In large organizations, the larger problem is irresolution and stasis; large mistakes on large matters are rarely mistakes of haste, but rather of delay or inaction.

The point of circulating promising people through varied and bigger jobs is to train and test them as they move along—in order to give them wide experience and confidence. As they climb higher, they should not automatically need ever more staff studies to do precisely what they've demonstrated they can do with little or less staff below. In the upper organizational echelons they should not be deprived of precisely those talents of quick insightfulness and confident decisiveness that moved them upward.

31

In organizational matters, few things are as bad as breeding people to managerial routines that equate order with rationality and careful study with true knowledge. Much staff work and many management reports are important, but usually they grow excessive and produce a dangerous inutility. Managers who come to believe themselves comfortably informed by the filtered information of completed staff work are both self-deluding and wrongly dependent.

As the manager rises ever higher, it takes greater effort to stay in solid contact with the things about which decisions must be made. To be able to make decisions with agile and easy confidence—in short, to inspire and lead—is a precondition of command. All else is mere administration.

7

The Mixed Metrics of Greed

GREED IS BORING. Everybody is against it, especially in public. We used to be more specific, against only "excessive" greed and in favor of something called "healthy" greed. Now both have been banished by the lofty eminences of various business roundtables. One is distasteful and the other oxymoronic.

Dennis B. Levine, once in certain recent times everybody's favorite villain after Ivan the Terrible, said, following a suitable period of public contrition, that trading on insider information was considered, until all the fuss, something of an occupational fringe benefit, like the delicatessen counterman's slipping home a little pastrami at night—more or less expected and widely indulged.

Well, maybe, except for the slight difference that Levine didn't take it home openly on the subway, wrapped in butcher paper. He flew off stealthily with tickets paid in cash, to make disguised deposits in a bank that traded secretly for his secret account. The law clearly said the dalliance was illegal. The people said it was also greedy, presumably because he was doing pretty well in what was regarded as an otherwise honorable profession by at least a marginal majority of the population.

Is that what greed is—the dirty secret of hidden avarice? If it's not systematically secreted from public view, is it then okay? How do people disposed to this kind of moral taxonomizing characterize such visibly devout acquisitors as T. Boone Pickens, Henry Kravis, David Murdoch, Mary Tyler Moore, Tom Peters, Bill Cosby, Adnan Khashoggi, and the multitudinous small fry like Harry the slumlord?

For some people, making money is, like weaving and cabinetmaking, a craft, but it is also a game. Sometimes they keep score by how much they make in one blow, like the little tailor in the fairy tale. Donald P. Kelly paid himself $6.75 million for helping structure the buyout of Beatrice Companies. A year later, as chairman of BCI Holdings Corporation, which did the buyout, he paid himself a $13 million salary. Another $277 million came his way later as profit. All this in about two years. Eat your heart out, Dennis Levine, rewarded for your entrepreneurship only with free room and board—and temporary, at that—in Lewisburg, Pennsylvania.

Money has three troublesome characteristics, and these do not ordinarily discriminate by age, gender, race, religion, national origin, breeding, or sexual preference: it is scarce, difficult to acquire, and transient. Before you know it, it's gone, and the less you have, the sooner you know it. That is why nearly everybody treats it respectfully. And why most people want more. Though we may believe fervently that some people already have enough (or even too much), they are neither obliged nor likely to agree. Their reasons are many, but what is commonly called greed is unlikely to be one of them and is, in any case, irrelevant.

Everybody marches to some tune, wants things in certain magnitudes and mixes, and pursues them in proportions commensurate with his or her energies and will. The person who is especially ardent in pursuit of money is widely disparaged for greediness, yet has much in common with those who with similar resoluteness pursue fame in the arts, acclaim in the professions, political attainment, organizational rank, social standing, or romantic conquest. Even those who work ardently for the belief that less is more may be said to be greedy for something, namely less.

Exceptional performers in sport, music, and dance are especially admired for their concentrated singlemindedness in training, study, practice, and performance. This is favorably known as dedication, discipline, focus, commitment . . . all for self-improvement and mastery.

People similarly dedicated to mastery in the pursuit of money are consecrated with no such approbation. The difference, presumably, is that self-enrichment replaces more virtuous pursuits or, more especially, that it occurs at someone else's expense. This same reasoning requires disparaging Ivan Lendl and Mikhail Baryshnikov for also succeeding, as it were, at the expense of others, unless one

35

insists that their means are fair while the means of moneymaking must necessarily be foul.

Socially it matters not who wins at tennis or ballet, whether Ted Williams or Ty Cobb was the better batter, or whether either was a better baseball player than the great pitchers of their times. Similarly, does it follow that it makes no social difference whether Warren Buffett or Ivan Boesky made millions for themselves mostly by betting, each in his own way, on companies they neither created nor managed? If Boesky's means had been socially acceptable, would it have made any difference?

Think of other realms. Is there a moral difference between coveting acclaim in the literary community, esteem in the local community, power in the world community, or position in the business community? And is it only "coveting" that is offensive—as in "Thou shalt not covet thy neighbor's wife"? Hardly, since this commandment follows another: "Thou shalt not commit adultery." The wish gets separate but equal disapproval with the deed.

There is also the matter of motive. Consider the notion that the artist should be accorded special treatment, including tax-free grants and generalized reverence. It is widely held that artists deliver a unique social benefit, derived from working, one supposes, only for art's higher purposes and not for selfish gain. Yet one hears W. H. Auden say, speaking of lyric poets such as himself, "They are not dependent, as people imagine, on feeling, inspiration, love, moonlight, despair; but are craftsmen who, like anybody else, earn honest money by working for a market. . . . " Or, consider the commercial sound of Sergei Prokofiev: "Art, like any other craft, has value only in the eyes of its consumer." Does all this matter? Should we distinguish between the artist and the art, the deed and the doer?

It is not by accident that the especially duplicitous financial manipulator is called a con *artist*. The artist is occupationally engaged in manipulating literality for purposes of persuasion and seduction. He or she seeks to affect and influence others, just as do the professor, the preacher, the panhandler, and the product pitchman.

Should the performer's motives color the deed's worthiness? Consider good deeds—social, civic, professional, cultural, and the like. Though they are widely acclaimed as being good, it is generally inadvisable for their performers to be conspicuously self-promotional. Ostentation is deeply disparaged. Gratitude and esteem are withheld from those who try indelicately to "buy their way in," especially with funds of unseemly origin. Both motive and money enter into our judgment of the deed's worthiness, especially the age of the money. New money is sometimes suspected, and occasionally even rejected, for being unsanitary. Old money is always judged hygienic, and therefore welcome.

It is useful to consider the Hebraic and the Hellenic approaches to judgment. The Hellenic makes moral and ethical judgments based on circumstance and motive. Things are relative and conditional. Judgment between difficult and conflicting claims is agonizing. It requires courage and virtue, the stuff of drama. By contrast the Hebraic standard is simple, absolute, unyielding—things are either right or wrong, good or evil. There are no inner struggles, no dilemmas, no hard choices, no ironies, no destinies. Moral-

37

ity is not drama. There is no wrestling with conscience or circumstance. There is only duty, duty to do what's obviously and absolutely right.

Neither way has proved entirely satisfying. Both of them work and don't work. Sin is definitionally reprehensible but not often absolutely definable. Thus, while no known society admires or approves of avarice or philistine self-promotion, all acknowledge and indulge a deep human tendency to look after Number One. Both tendencies reign; neither can be totally reined in.

In common usage, greed refers to wantonness, to excess in the service of what is itself excessive. But it is an elastic metric, resolutely Hellenic. Even the great Rabbi Hillel of the First Common Era waffled: "If I am not for myself, who is for me?" he wrote in a much quoted phrase. Less quoted is his continuation: "but if I am for my own self only, what am I, and if not now, when?" This is not a declarative statement, nor entirely an admonition. It is a counsel of moderation, in behavior as well as in how we judge it. It is also a call to conscience. It condones self-interest, but not its intemperate or perverse expressions—such as grasping acquisitiveness, sleaziness, charlatanism, deceit, or even inordinate narcissism.

In the end, distinctions must be made. Not all forms of self-interest are equal. Not all obsessively narrow dedications to mastery and attainment are equally admirable or reprehensible. Honest greed—whether for money, acclaim, or conquest—is not axiomatically an oxymoron. It makes a certain useful contribution to getting the world's work done.

8

Rascality and Virtue

THERE IS a marvelous periodicity to the nation's major concerns. In business and in politics it has converged in recent years on the ethics of people in high places.

In its closing apotheosis, the Reagan White House was caught flagrante delicto in a scam about which it professed innocence and sought, against overwhelming odds, to finesse suspicions with which even the president's mother might have had some difficulties.

With little effort, in one lifetime in America we can recall President Nixon's Watergate, President Eisenhower's vicuna coat, President Truman's similar unfortunateness about a freezer similarly given to a similarly intimate high-level adviser, and, of course, the Teapot Dome episode in

President Warren Gamaliel Harding's complacent White House.

It is not such a long distance from Pennsylvania Avenue to Wall Street, where Ivan Boesky, the celebrated miscreant, was paraded before the public with ill-gotten dollars dribbling from his pockets. And, of course, that's not new either. Not so long before Boesky there were such memorable rascals as Marc Rich, Robert Vesco, Billy Sol Estes, and, further back, Richard Whitney, who went from the New York Stock Exchange, where as president he'd been the pillar of Establishment rectitude, directly to residency in Sing Sing prison for deeds judged despicable precisely because of his ancient lineage and august position. Boesky is, by that standard, a low-rent-district knave.

No matter. What would the public do for titillation and amusement without such deliciously gossipy sordidness? Without it, how would we be reminded of our ethical duties and cautioned about our moral vulnerabilities? How would we otherwise confirm our superior merit over those who squirm before our scandalized eyes?

Few things are so satisfying as the warming righteousness attendant on witnessing some especially outrageous rascality committed by persons in positions of great trust or in one's close professional proximity. The experience confers a certain flushed distinction, like having emerged honored and unscathed from some terribly bloody battle in the service of homeland and virtue.

Still, in the twilight moments before falling asleep in one's bed at night, the thought subversively intrudes that there, but for the grace of God, might have gone *I*. To have been privately close but publicly spared may be, for some, exhilarating, like speedboat racing. For most it's probably deeply discomforting, remindful of their own privy violations of the complete code of ethical hygiene.

Absolution is unavailable. There remains only the thought that absolute incorruptibility in matters of ethics and morality ranks with chastity as one of life's great probabilistic aberrations, and that if it prevailed, large armies of people in both sacred and secular occupations would go unemployed.

The world of work is a world of warring wits. Even the swarming anthill, where all are genetically programmed for utopian cooperation, turns out on close examination to be a perennial struggle for advantage by all, each obsessively trying to get there quickly before the other deposits an impediment.

The world of work is normally no more dangerous to one's ethical health than the world of play or prayer. Nor is work in a competitive environment any more or less safe or corrupting than in a cooperative or communal setting.

A common tale told immemorially by all religions refers to humankind's fall from grace. None say it happened either in the marketplace, in the chambers of the polity, or in literary salons. Instead, the tale explains, it happened in a garden, in paradise. Presumably neither cash nor competition existed there to entice or corrupt—only curiosity. Yet paradise was not a free-goods society—the forbidden fruit was gotten at a price.

9

Convictions

The Organization

An organization is not a mob. It may be nicely participative, but not democratic. It is hierarchical by necessity, but everything else is by choice, chance, indifference, or neglect.

The Manager's Career

Nothing so damages a manager's career as the casual comment that sometimes he or she has a little trouble making decisions.

Action vs. Talk

The necessity of action cannot be avoided by flight into rhetoric or retreat into analysis.

Executive Energy

Inaction is the only inexhaustible form of executive energy.

The Memorandum

The memorandum has been transformed from a means to inform the receiver into an instrument to promote the sender. This change has been much welcomed at Xerox.

Listening

The effective manager develops the ability to hear what others are not saying.

The Effective Subordinate

The effective subordinate exceeds the expectations of superiors, protects their reputations, and gives them all the credit.

Rank and Authority

Rank is an appointed position. Authority is an earned condition. Rank is decreed from above. Authority is conferred from below. Authority vanishes the moment those who bestowed it stop believing, respecting, or trusting their appointed boss, though they may defer out of fear.

Title

A person may hold a title long after having ceased to function effectively in it.

Looking vs. Seeing

People decline in energy as they advance in years. Some make up with experience and wisdom what they have lost in vitality and agility. But at all ages people commonly mistake the mirror for the window.

What Gets Done

Because something can be done, it usually gets done. To acknowledge this is to shift from constraining convictions about what is immutable to healthy consideration of what is possible. It liberates the imagination from self-deluding beliefs of what must be and self-denying fears of what might be.

Ideas and Deeds

Ideas are not good enough. Ideas are not deeds. Ideas are rarely converted into action unless proselytized with zeal, carried with passion, sustained by conviction, and fortified by faith. They need authentic champions. Above all, ideas need people who are doers, not just talkers.

Change and Decisions

Bernoulli's principle explains that the faster a gas or fluid flows, the less pressure it exerts. This helps explain a lot of bad decisions in management. The more convincingly managers think they are surrounded by a lot of rapid change, the more they will merely react and the less they will think.

Attitudes

In business, as in much else, success comes mostly to those who attack each task with the passion of the scientist and the precision of the artist.

On Target

Whenever you hear that everything is going as planned, somebody is either a fool or a liar.

Electrons and Customers

Physics says that an electron is whatever physicists know about the electron. By extension, are we to suppose that what we know about customers is what professional market researchers say? Hardly. Managers must know things directly for themselves, must go out there where the warm armpits are.

Administration vs. Management

The administrator sees that the work is done right. The manager, that the right work is done. Both are needed.

Neither is superior to the other, though the latter is scarcer than the former.

Doing Management

The practice of management is badly misunderstood by management scientists who confuse thinking with merely being logical.

Marketing and Maladies

Marketing power is related to how well competitors metabolize information to their advantage. Companies that don't metabolize information right will see small problems and discontinuities metastasize into major maladies.

Forecasting

The future is not the linear extrapolation of the present. The world does not move on perfectly parallel railroad tracks laid down by rational social engineers. Humankind intervenes. But the result is rarely what was intended. Fortunately, a benign Providence has contrived that usually there is just enough time before it is too late.

Change and Inertia

Though change is everywhere, more things endure than don't. We have an irresistible tendency to equate superficial changes with fundamental revisions, to mistake incidents for trends and activity for movement, to see connections everywhere while making distinctions nowhere. We are helped ahead more by agility than prescience and as much by perseverance as ability, and we are saved from folly by the inertia that facilitates most of the world's work. In our advanced years, may we all return finally to Springfield and make popcorn by the fire.

TWO

Changing

10

Betterness

MOST THINGS get done in small doses. "Every day in every way I'm getting better and better," goes the inspirational mantra. Japanese business language speaks prescriptively of *kaizen,* continuous improvement. Trying routinely to get better one step at a time is a far better way to get better than shooting constantly for the moon.

Major prophetic leaps into sudden business success are rare. That is why they make the headlines, as do similarly sudden and spectacular flops. Sustained success is largely a matter of focusing regularly on the right things and making a lot of uncelebrated little improvements every day. Getting better and better one step at a time adds up. Sometimes a little step turns surprisingly into a big leap. Occasionally there will be big or daring efforts in pursuit of big results that, even more surprisingly, actually pay off. In these combinations of ways, big powerhouse corporations finally get built. It is also how they stay strong and ahead—how they become the blue-chip companies we wisely prefer to have our retirement pensions invested in.

The fact that strong big companies regularly spend a lot on R&D and on new products and new ventures, or even have big setbacks, is not entirely beside the point. By doing a lot of things well and trying constantly to do them a little better, they generate the cash and build the confidence to try occasional big things without jeopardizing the whole enterprise.

The world of affairs is certifiably unstable and largely unpredictable. Almost nothing lasts, especially if it's a good thing. What's called excellence today is apt to be execrable tomorrow. Things wear out. Strategies and programs exhaust themselves. And what doesn't actually wear out gets caught up with and passed by. People tire and slow down—no matter that they get briefly aroused at inspirational convocations to go passionately after an undefined and unsustainable excellence. Inevitably, manufactured inspiration collapses into disappointment, cynicism, and retreat. The messiah of excellence, defrocked by failure, turns vehemently against rationality, and in unctuous conceits pronounces the world chaotic.

An organization succeeds through thick and thin by operating according to simple principles and beliefs that can be comprehended and sustained under the pressures, push, and boredom of life's daily duties and routines. The organization that succeeds has a constant curiosity about its customers and competitors. It aims for reasonable attainments that its members can have some direct impact on and get some modest recognition for. It asks of them neither heroism nor miracles, and certainly not theatrics. It seeks and eagerly rewards honest workmanship, committed effort, and innovation.

Years ago at 3M, a product manager who later became a high executive said, "We try a lot and do a lot of things, a little of this and a little of that, and try to make it work. We make a little and sell a little; then make and sell a little more and a little better. Usually, something pretty good happens. It can even get big. And all along we know who did what and who we are."

Things may not be that homespun in other solid and achieving companies, but the spirit is much the same— progress by *kaizen,* by modestly attainable increments. That helps explain Tide's hammerlock market share these past thirty years, Bisquick's endurance through thick and thin, Sony's continuous flow of successful new products, and the persistence of Siemens and so many other blue-chip corporations.

Everybody at every level keeps intelligently and diligently at work, attending to the issues and details appropriate to his or her job. Everybody tries always to do even the little things in new and better ways, without any presumption of having to make rockets go off in the evening skies. There are no special heroes, only honest journeymen with solid work habits and good instincts. Everybody tries every day to do things a little better and get better results. Effort and vision build, little by little, into a cumulating momentum. Success gets sustained by cultivating, largely via planning, budgeting, and management, healthy habits of constructive self-examination and environmental awareness.

53

Improving things little by little does not mean sticking wrongly to what should no longer be done. Without a market in suitable abundance, nothing works. No amount of betterness can reverse Sol Hurok's immutable law: "When people don't want to come, nothing in the world will stop them."

Betterness comes in all magnitudes, but it is not likely to come in any sustainable proportion if unsustainable efforts are wrongly urged on the organization. What is surely unhealthful is to invite raging evangelists periodically to whip people into believing the latest fast fixes.

11

Innovation

NEVER LEAVE well enough alone. Others certainly won't, and that affects everybody. That is why it is more important to ask "What's new?" than "How's business?"—"How's business?" is about the past, but "What's new?" is about the future. There is nothing you can do about the past—about what has already happened—but you can do something about the future and what might happen.

What's new can either help or hurt you. Everybody should be attentive to it. And everybody should try to develop the ability to interpret the pace, direction, meaning, and significance of what's happening. Not everything that's happening is new, nor does it necessarily equate with change. One should learn to understand the difference between an event and a trend. Some things are merely occasions, passing blips on the screen of time. They are not genuinely transformational in substance, sustainability, or likelihood.

Likelihood is a good criterion, because not everything that is possible is probable. More things endure than change—and the more sudden and visible an event or occasion, the greater the likelihood that it is only temporary and therefore not significantly transformational.

To ascertain the likelihood of a forecasted event, one should always ask, "What else has to happen for that to happen?" Thus there is the much prognosticated office of the future—people working on networked computers at home rather than commuting "wastefully" to the office. But what else has to happen for that to happen? Will the quality of work at home be sustainable without the physical, emotional, and conversational presence of colleagues gathered institutionally together specifically for work? Can any group of adults ever actually function professionally in a social setting that is designed specifically for family living and child development rather than for work? Will all these have to change in order to make the computer-networked home worker effective?

The market economy evolved from the natural disposition of people to help themselves—either as creators and sellers of what others wanted, or as buyers of what others created or sold. As long as people are reasonably free to follow their own inclinations, there will be innovation, because they will find ways to offer improvements on what is already available for people to buy, and ways to buy faster, cheaper, and more congenially. Nobody ever leaves well enough alone, except maybe those who are exhausted or disabled.

That means that innovation is an axial characteristic of markets. But because organizations evolve to do predictable work, they create procedures and routines that also tend to stifle innovation. Innovation may be systematically fostered by organized R&D and managed change, but mostly fixed procedures and set routines impede change.

That is why one of the chief duties of managers is to encourage their people and their organizations to think imaginatively and act aggressively—even to smash the constraints of the required routines and circumvent the systems over which they preside.

To break the cake of custom, to take nothing for granted, never to leave well enough alone, to ask always "Why not?" "What else?" "How else?" "Who else?" and *again* "Why not?"—these are among the manager's most important duties; and also to perform with efficient and predictable reliability, day in and day out, the necessary repetitive tasks prescribed by the routines that have been laid down organizationally.

No amount of low-cost production or high-yield selling is good enough in the service of what is not itself good enough. Nothing is more wasteful than doing with great efficiency that which should not be done at all. The constant in business that must be done is innovation everywhere in the organization, at all its levels, and regarding all its tasks. That is the only way the constantly expanding requirements of markets can be served. If it is not done, no company can long survive, no matter how low-cost its production.

12

The Youthification of Management

WE DECLINE in energy as we advance in years. So do managers. But pressures on managers mount as things change, and especially as change accelerates. That is no time for waning energies.

As with the professions of engineering and medicine, what management does has to work, and what works has to be right. The determination of what is right—what to do—is largely the province of wisdom, which comes with experience and age. Doing it right and making it work are the province of energy, endurance, agility, optimism, and even daring. These are the special qualities of youth.

As competition gets intensified by the rising pace of newness, the work of management will increasingly have to be done by those most capable of operating in that environment—that is, by a younger generation.

People in business clearly believe that business has become more complex, global, and knowledge driven—not "is becoming," but "has become." They also think the opposite—that sometimes we just make it seem complex, and that we need to return to simple basics; that businesses have entirely too many scorekeepers, money changers, and analysts, and too few real workers and activists; that while business has become more specialized, it increasingly needs managers who are powerful generalists. Managers need to know more—and, in a funny way, also less. The feeling is that there is a lot of wasteful attentiveness to stuff that's irrelevant, silly, and trivial; that instead of working harder in accustomed old ways we need to work smarter in elegant new ways; that technology drives more of everything we do, but also that this makes more important than ever the proper training, motivation, and treatment of people.

The manager's most precious and least manageable commodity is time. Reports and data pile up faster and higher, but information is harder to get—and harder still to get meaning out of, even though colleagues and staff constantly suggest lots of meaning.

Then there are the communications from the outside that constantly claim the manager's attention—magazines, trade reports, studies, newsletters, and so forth. Close by are clamoring experts, consultants, scholars, seminars, conferences, and cassettes. Journalists and jingoists, smelling new markets, package fictional trends, imagined waves, motivational concoctions, and simplifying formulas, paradigms, and managerial fads into saleable products. All promise salvation, liberation from the necessity to think for oneself. All compete for the time and minds of busy and burdened people who are already saturated with more data and ideas than they can use.

These entrepreneurs have institutionalized change, news of change, and how to manage change. It is in their interest that change must be seen as ubiquitous, trends as palpable, the future predictable, and things so misty and confused as to require expert interpretation and guidance. Things must get whipped into a breathless whirl, unsettled, chaotic, confounding, confusing, perplexing. In that way supply creates its own demand.

And business literature turns increasingly to merchandising, to glitz, gossip, sensationalism, one-minute miracles, and walking-around homilies—all breathlessly hyped and technicolored to cover over the thin, insubstantial, and insufficient.

But liberation languishes. New management tools and operating routines purportedly designed to solve management problems usually just expand and intensify the problems. And that is a certain formula for getting people to feel their age.

Most people feel their age too soon. They decline in years before they actually retire. The approximate state of aging has little to do with age itself. Aging is a journey, a matter of how you feel rather than how long you've traveled. Few of us can be the age we really want to be. And, of course, youth itself cannot last. Not everybody can be young, though being youthful is within everybody's reach. Youth is a temporal phase; youthfulness a psychological condition.

Mature managers are, these days, getting to feel entirely too mature too fast. Early retirement is not just the growing consequence of declining capability in a rapidly changing world, but of growing feelings of growing pressures. Instead of merely *being* assaulted by technological acceleration, market intensification, the globalization of competition, and the hostile rattlings of unfamiliar predators, managers increasingly *feel* assaulted, also cornered and even confused. Long-used industry definitions have gotten rapidly scrambled and boundaries extended. Familiar managerial routines and practices somehow work less reliably. Marauding outsiders upset established relationships. Colleagues seem less congenial, subordinates less tractable. New laws and social activists intrude. Decision-making gets harder about everything: capital allocation, selection, training, disciplining, and motivation of people, which markets to enter, abandon, milk, or pursue, which technologies and investments to back, and whether to expand vigorously, bide one's time, retrench, or build reserves against adversity. And the libido, well, it's not what it used to be.

Across the street, the grass seems somehow greener. In many other industries and places, especially in the newer and technologically more intense, younger managers and entrepreneurs and specialists seem to predominate. In fact, everywhere the young seem to swim with confident ease in what their experienced elders think is hazardous turbulence.

61

Greater abundances of energy, ability, confidence, and libido are, by definition, characteristics of the young. The young have a special advantage in a rapidly changing world, even though they have less industry knowledge, less familiarity with what's gone before, and less knowledge about the ways of organizations, people, and competitors. Because they are not likely to have the wisdom that only deep experience confers, they may be more easily bamboozled by plausible simplifiers and elegant technocrats, and misled by their own hubris.

It is therefore understandable that those whom accelerating times drive early into feelings of middle or advanced managerial age sometimes get annoyed by the fast attainments, impatience, presumptions, and swagger of the young. Still, the young are generally more adept, agile, confident, and entrepreneurial, especially in such times. They are remarkably fast learners, even of some tricks it has been said only old dogs can learn.

Business success requires being compatible with the environment. This is especially appreciated where the pace of technology, competition, and events is intense. It explains IBM's celebrated rule that its officers relinquish their titles at age sixty. It explains the disproportionate upper-echelon presence of the young in the booming new industries—electronics, genetic engineering, software, fast food, specialty retailing, entertainment, travel, various service organizations, and mergers and acquisitions. In all things, being youthful helps, but in some it is absolutely better to be young. We know this to be so in the hostile environments of warfare. It is also true of intensely competitive and rapidly changing business conditions.

Organizations cannot be kept vigorous or be revitalized simply by restructuring or resorting to faddish indulgences. They cannot be helped by "introducing a new corporate culture," by reciting the magical mantras of a best-seller business book, by adopting the easy plausibilities of evangelical zealots on the speakers' circuit, or applying, however carefully, fixed scholastic formulas. The only fix is systemic. That usually means new blood—mostly the blood of people younger than those long in the upper ranks.

Younger people should be moved sooner into positions of responsibility and command, where they can be trained, stretched, tested, and mentored so that organizations can benefit from the special prowess they bring to these special times.

13

The Innovating
Organization

ORGANIZATIONS EXIST to enable ordinary people to do extraordinary things. To accomplish this end they must routinize their work. Precisely because of that, the purposes for which organizations exist cause organizations to decline in their ability to achieve their purposes.

Routinization of anything is self-immolating. It deadens alertness, attentiveness, imagination, energy, and reaction time. Wherever routine reigns, special effort is needed to sustain attention and responsiveness, to energize the system and its functionaries, to freshen the mind and get people moving. That is why peacetime armies require continuing education for their managerial cadres, why the more successful large corporations have frequent reorganizations and restructurings. With these, established procedures and relationships get questioned and disrupted, people get reassigned, tasks get redefined, minds get newly engaged, old problems get fresh attention, new ones get discovered, and innovation gets stimulated. An organization whose operating efficiency requires the deep routinization of any significant part of its work achieves agility and resourcefulness only by special efforts.

Leadership in the self-renewing and thriving enterprise is characterized by its willingness to move beyond tidy models of what leadership is and does. Leaders establish order and discipline, and simultaneously foster skepticism, incredulity, experimentation, and change. They encourage the generation of new forms and actions that may have neither precedent nor accustomed approval. They inject creative enzymes into the system, with results that can be destabilizing and disorderly and are rarely parametric. They know that to achieve more and better results, more resourcefulness is as important as more resources.

In most organizations, the really new things get accomplished mostly by subterfuge and cunning. They get started in the organizational underground and interstices, and are financed largely by diversions and sweat. They go public only when successful, or because of calamity.

The effectively functioning organization makes change its open ally. It keeps the barriers low. Its leaders know that survival and strength require the periodic euthanasia of the organization's accustomed routines. Otherwise everybody and everything winds down. Entropy overtakes enterprise. Competitiveness diminishes and finally expires.

Nothing characterizes the successful organization so much as its willingness to abandon what has been long successful. Of course, not all that is new is better. Good things have good reasons for enduring. It may be good to be skeptical of fashionable new prescriptions for achieving organizational vitality and competitive virtuosity, but it's bad to be resistant to the kind of healthy self-examination that might prescribe new medicine.

Nobody who leads or manages knowingly resists self-examination and adaptation. But to keep the barriers low takes effort. It requires open advocacy and demonstrable receptiveness to innovation. The history of long-surviving and thriving enterprises is a history of innovation, mostly by their forcing changes on others and on themselves. Sometimes these occur suddenly and painfully. Mostly they happen gradually, continuously, even imperceptibly. What's key, especially in the complex organization where work is deeply regularized, is leadership that insists on constant open self-examination of everything, on receptiveness to change, and on the budgetary encouragement of innovation. It seeks out, encourages, and supports intelligent, experienced people who have the will, energy, and courage to make changes they think make sense. Often these people will be younger rather than older.

Precisely because so much of the world's work can be effectively and reliably done only by the large routinizing organization, it is there that leadership needs to be especially innovative.

14

On Agility and Stability

A HUGE publishing and educational industry thrives on the proposition that the creative core of business resides predominantly among smaller and newer companies; that the larger established ones are hopelessly bureaucratic, lethargic, and unimaginative; and that spectacular opportunity awaits anybody with energy, determination, and a little leverage.

This increasingly fashionable hype has some plausibility, and actually signifies a nicely succeeding society. Only where opportunity is available to the undistinguished many, and not limited to the privileged few, will there be an authentic market for its commercialization. The existence of a large continuing market for the entrepreneurial promise signifies a society in which the facts justify its existence.

But it is easy to exaggerate what small new firms do. Their economic importance is obvious. Yet remarkably few actually possess exceptional enterprise or new ideas. Mostly they are imitative, repeating what others have already done. Mostly they represent modest attempts to attain independence and self-employment via well-established routes. Few last long, and fewer thrive. Many are simply the illusionary creations of people seeking employment they cannot otherwise find or escapes from industrial disciplines they cannot abide.

New ventures and new creations in large corporations are rarely noted or even recognized as being new, unless they are especially magnificent, gigantic, or larcenous. Yet newness of considerable importance is a regular occurrence in almost all large corporations.

Because large firms generally serve mature markets with relatively stable sales, they are sensibly advised to focus on doing new things that improve efficiency rather than things that are dramatically dissimilar and disproportionate. Still, innovation is an essential and central activity of all large firms, though it will not be as visible there as in small firms that are organized specifically to do new things.

Last year IBM spent $6 billion on R&D, none of it for pizza shops or monster toys. Merck spent $500 million, and USX $50 million on its steel operations alone. Some celebrated innovations followed, but mostly the yield was hidden from the public, consisting largely of ways to raise efficiency and improve competitiveness. They hardly qualified as juicy journalism.

The infant grows more rapidly than the child. That is not an argument against the child and says nothing about the greater merit of being young or small—or large, more settled, and more experienced. There is no presumption that the agility of the gazelle is superior or preferable to the stability of the elephant, or vice versa. Du Pont spent $167 million (in today's dollars) over a ten-year period on a single project before finally getting back a dime with nylon. Genentech is a magnificent tribute to the gazelle, but it had to get quickly larger in order to do its important new things. It got that large only with the venture capital support of very large companies.

Nearly all today's big established companies were yesterday's upstarts. Some of tomorrow's creative newness will come from today's small start-ups. That is how a well-functioning society works. The nation that does not lower ladders of economic opportunity to the young and to enterprise is fated to failure. So is the nation that hobbles or discredits the large enterprises whose organizing skills, productive prowess, and huge investments create so much unacknowledged innovation, efficiency, and stability, and which help produce the capital and support the markets that encourage and sustain new companies.

The world's work gets done by all sizes of enterprise. None is constitutionally superior to any other. Enterprises of different sizes each do differently needed and different newly imagined things. All can be—and are—gazelle-like in their own special ways. What really happens in this big complex world is that enterprise thrives largely where variety is enabled and encouraged to be and become what the march of events requires it to be and become.

15

Fast History

MORE THAN ever before, business survival and success require getting compatible with a rapidly arriving and disruptive future, but a future that cannot be specifically foretold.

Though forecasting specific events is futile, becoming conversant in the growing technical language and comfortable with the evolving conditions and events that shape the future is an increasingly essential part of what management is and does. Managers who don't make the effort, who don't learn, and who don't get comfortable with what needs to be learned will surely constrain their careers and hurt their companies.

Things change and always have changed. Fast history is an environment of intensifying and unexpected changes, of rapid acceleration. This creates special problems and also special opportunities.

Indeed, it has become cliché to say that newness creates both problems and opportunities. The result is that this common observation actually intensifies the acceleration to which it refers. One of the central activities of modern management has become change itself—making change, making big and often drastic changes, being organizationally geared for change, and quickly responding to changes made by others. Everything is suddenly up for grabs, a candidate for intense scrutiny and questioning. Nothing is exempt from the presumption that it is alterable or excisable.

Nowhere is this more the case than in the maturer industries, the ones that over the years have changed relatively little but have now become so vulnerable to predators and reorganizers.

Change has certain self-masking and therefore delusionary qualities. Sometimes it takes years to realize we lived through some very big disruptions and transformations. And we have trouble distinguishing an incident from a trend, an event from a climacteric. Though deeply transforming changes are relatively rare, change is now more ubiquitous than most people acknowledge and certainly more than they find comfortable or manageable. That helps explain nostalgia—the sentimental yearning for an imagined and idyllic past, a time of order, stability, gradualism, predictability, respectfulness, and courtesy, even of innocence. People always want to get back to what they never had.

What we have we usually get slowly. Changes that affect business generally creep up quietly, on cat's paws, little noticed until later, when they can really hurt. But in business as in life, heavy turbulence and eruptions are infrequent, which makes them no less hurtful. Stability and gradualism are actually the norm, which is how to get complacent.

Accepted wisdom has it that change is now for the first time driven by dramatic and frequent developments in science and technology. This is a wisdom light on historical knowledge. Better memory recalls the turbulence and devastation of the early days of railroading, telephones, steel, oil, electric motors, chemicals, automobiles, the radio. So strong is the compulsion to extinguish or romanticize past unpleasantness and so compelling the inclination to make today's times seem especially challenging that even the bloodied participants in the two relatively recent shakeouts in television manufacturing have forgotten the awful details.

But one thing that's now uniquely new is the intensity of the semiconductor explosion. It touches and transforms everything—rapidly, convulsively, and conclusively, even the practice of management itself. And though it is true that much the same can be said of the steam engine, the telephone, the variable-horsepower electric motor, and the automobile, "much the same" is not "exactly the same." Semiconductor electronics is substantively different—infinitely more versatile, more deeply embedded in things and operations, more powerfully systematic in the changes it makes and facilitates—and it accelerates faster, transforms itself faster, and travels the world more quickly and decisively.

Not everything changes, and certainly not everything changes constantly. Actually, more things abide than don't. But in the new age of fast history, the things that don't abide will more quickly than ever damage, and even destroy, companies that are slow to make change their ally.

16

Deliriums of Entrepreneurship

Entrepreneur is one of those alluring French words, like *cuisine* and *haute couture,* that take over everywhere, regardless of country. In our own country, the entrepreneur is now lyricized everywhere for accomplishments and possibilities once reserved only for mythic figures.

Two distinct parts make up the ballyhoo, one sacred, the other secular. Wrote an especially infatuated apostle: "The entrepreneurial sacrifice is a religious experience. Entrepreneurs give wholly of themselves, sacrificing everything—their time, their marriages, their assets, and their sleep—for their private, tenacious belief in a redemptive idea." Powerful stuff.

What exactly is that idea? Is it to be, curiously, like the hippies of the unlamented past, free from social and economic encumbrances? Here are the actual printed words of another febrile convert: "For at least the first year of my liberation [from the corporation], there was not a day in which I did not actually revel in the fact that I had stepped into a realm where time had an extra dimension."

Characterized by such delirium, entrepreneurship was the sacred mushroom of the 1980s. It seemed delusively greater and grander than it was. In some circles it converted into a theology complete with commentaries like George Gilder's *The Spirit of Enterprise*. In other circles it sounded remarkably secular, even fashionable—it was the thing to do, to be celebrated for doing—and it had its own how-to periodicals like *Inc., Venture, Savvy,* and *Black Enterprise.* (Even large corporations were bamboozled into preaching the latest, and perhaps ugliest, management neologism, "intrapreneurship.")

Both circles, the priests and the promoters, celebrated liberation from the constraining regularity of conventional employment. Like their antiestablishment cousins of the 1960s, both also celebrated the higher validity of smallness over bigness, and yet, with acrobatic versatility, both linked entrepreneurship tightly to the idea of making money, lots of it. It is fitting that France, homeland of the big word, is now homeland of its biggest prophet, Bernard Tappie. On his popular television program, "Ambition," and in his best-selling autobiography, *Winning,* he preaches, "Create companies and earn big money through entrepreneurship. . . . Dare to think big."

But now that the idea of entrepreneurism has persisted in being fashionable, there's nothing particularly daring

74

about thinking big and acquisitively while simultaneously preaching self-reliance, small enterprise, and selflessness. When things become commonplace, casuists materialize like mushrooms on a damp day to offer absolution and moral legitimacy.

None of this is particularly new. Just consider Benjamin Franklin's *Poor Richard's Almanac,* or Bruce Barton's hugely successful inspirational success book of 1925, *The Man Nobody Knows,* or Richard G. Conwell's crisscrossing of the nation in 1915 to deliver his famous commercially redemptive speech, "Acres of Diamonds."

If entrepreneurship was the hippie youth of the 1980s, then making money was its long hair. That too became authentically fashionable, like being slim, patriotic, "sensitive," elegantly rugged like Ralph Lauren or tough like Rambo, being "into" jogging and weekending, switching to white wine, asserting that the Japanese made things better than anybody, and going crazy over the Superbowl.

Entrepreneurship is a capitalist idea par excellence. Surely it is better for America than even the Superbowl, and certainly it creates more jobs and probably more public pleasure each year than even Bill Cosby, certainly more than Larry Bird. It is the essential renewing stuff, part of what makes America continually great and helps explain capitalism's new popularity worldwide.

Not so great are the prophets of entrepreneurship who, practicing their own flashy brand of entrepreneurial hustle, profit from empty speeches about the liberating, ennobling, and profit-building possibilities of entrepreneurship for everybody; who'd have you think that all self-employment is also entrepreneurship, like sinking your life's savings into a banana-peeling franchise. If the entrepreneurship that is now so vigorously propagandized is not actually the false messiah of our economic times, certainly it is a falsified notion.

Everything in excess is a poison. A massive switch of the economy's ordinary journeymen into the new noble profession of entrepreneurship is unlikely, thank God. Who would reliably restock the shelves each day, thus ensuring dependability, continuity, and stability?

So, one exuberant cheer for entrepreneurship, but, lest we forget, two sober cheers for the unennobled rest of us who regularly do the laundry, give ourselves our daily bread, and make each morning predictably fresh and sunny all over again, even if it's just like yesterday.

17

Entrepreneuring Eastern Europe

AT THE OTHER END of the telephone, the confident stranger identified himself as being from Whatley & Chambers, as if everybody knew them. "We've heard you're interested in Poland. So is Humphrey Hubert, chairman of the Hilltop Group," he said, as if everybody knew them too, or that it mattered. "He'll be in Boston tomorrow night on his way to Moscow and would like to have dinner with you."

After many years and many regretted accommodations to such unwanted invitations, the listener would normally have politely declined this one as well.

This time, perhaps momentarily unbalanced by the thought that Poland could use all the help it was able to get, the listener quickly accepted—but the caller just as quickly said, "Fine, then, Mr. Hubert will expect your call in his room at the Meridien Hotel at nine tomorrow night." The listener was sorry, but that was too late. "I know it's late, sir, but Mr. Hubert has an important engagement in New York that afternoon and won't be able to leave earlier." Sorry. "Then perhaps you could see him for breakfast the next morning—say, seven-thirty?" Sorry, only for an early dinner tomorrow. "Let's see what we can do. I'll call back." When? "Well, he's a very busy man, you know. When do you need to know?" This being an invitation to demonstrate equivalent busyness, he got an equivalent answer: in fifteen minutes. In ten minutes he called back sealing the Meridien supper at seven P.M.

At seven P.M., Mr. Hubert answered his room call cheerfully. "I'll be down in two minutes sharp," he said. "I'm tall, slim, and fully gray-headed." All true. He was also full of easy congeniality. The tall, slim, fully gray head swiftly led the way to the mezzanine-floor restaurant.

At the table he spoke importantly of "my book," of his close friendships with various political eminences such as Pete and Mike and Henry and Jesse and Ben and so forth, of his business background, of his three prior important trips to the Soviet Union, and of his eagerness "to do as much for the Polish people." As much of what? Well, in Russia he'd met with "lots of important officials like, well, Mr. Smolisky, or something like that, chief of the planning economy." He'd also "traveled there extensively," "inspected" many factories, and had "many, many discussions" with their managers. And what had brought him there, especially to the factories (given that he'd apparently spent most of his business life refinancing bank-ruptcies in California)? "My convictions about entrepreneurship—which they really need and which I explain in my book," he said, concerning which he now had "this important invitation" to speak in Moscow.

Entrepreneurship . . . of course. But a few questions revealed that he'd not heard of the explosively multiplying number of Soviet so-called cooperatives, the euphemism for its couple of hundred thousand new private-enterprise, privately financed businesses, of the for-profit Soviet association of cooperatives, nor even of Vladimir Yakovlev, its ebullient and highly visible young president.

Would he perhaps like to visit Mr. Yakovlev? An introduction, perhaps? "Of course," he said, "but later, when there's more time." Right now he'd like to stop off in Poland "to see how I can help there too." And how might that be? "Explain entrepreneurship, of course."

Until then the tall, slim, fully gray-headed missionary up-from-New York, headed-for-Moscow, and eager-for-Warsaw, had not asked even a single question about his guest's Polish connections, interests, knowledge, activities, or intentions. Nor did he ask later, which came soon indeed. Suddenly, the host was on his feet, extending a firm handshake for "all the help and insight you've given me this evening."

Full of wonderment outside the Meridien, the guest was stimulated by the newspaper headlines to more wondering. If all these years of Communist rule did not kill the spirit of people in Eastern Europe, nor entirely destroy the Soviet people's entrepreneurial instincts, surely they would recognize this different kind of snake-oil salesman?

One hopes that sources of help and advice besides Mr. Hubert will get used in Eastern Europe, and especially that a lot of commissars and entrepreneurs are brothers under the skin. Otherwise, a lot of rubles and zlotys will be spent on potions nobody can afford and everybody will regret.

18

Futurism and Management

The following text is from a speech delivered at the annual lunch of the British-American Chamber of Commerce in London, June 5, 1989. Excluded are my opening remarks, intended largely to amuse the convening delegates into a state of undiscriminating receptivity, so that they might return to their offices believing that their well-lubricated midday repast was justified by the wisdom they had imbibed.

"We should all be concerned about the future because that's where we'll have to spend the rest of our lives." So said Charles F. Kettering, an old-fashioned automotive tinkerer who, though American, actually spoke in complete and comprehensible sentences.

We live in a world of rapid acceleration, of fast history. No longer does one ask "How's business?" but rather "What's new?" How things are is less important than how they might become, because what might be can either help or hurt you. What might be lies entirely in the future.

Careful study leads me to conclude that one of the problems with the future is that good things always take longer than they should, whereas bad things happen right away.

That is the secret professional futurologists know, which is why they don't speak of things that can happen right away. They speak exclusively of things far out, not near in. Far out they can safely offer salvation (good news, big booms), which they must do lest they fail on the lecture circuit, because nobody comes to lunch to hear bad news. Bad news back at the office is one reason you come to lunch—to escape from life as it really is day to day.

Back at Harvard we know something about life as it really is, which may surprise people familiar with universities in the United Kingdom. In 1959 one of our most illustrious Harvard professors published a famous book— *The Affluent Society*—and ever since, the world speaks mostly of poverty.

The English novelist P. H. Newby said of one of his characters, "If he'd been a Hebrew he would have prophesied, being English he spoke of his childhood." In your childhoods you may have heard of the New York World's Fair exposition of 1939. Its most popular and grandest exhibit was General Motor's Motorama. Prophetically it showed beautiful multiple-laned motorways, cloverleafs and roundabouts, confident and well-dressed adults and children driving contentedly in lovely tree-lined urban places—the places of the future.

Today, with technology booming, GNP everywhere in ascendance, with elegantly overpriced restaurants crowded with the self-consciously rich and the expense-account enriched, the producing cities of old are almost everywhere in shambles . . . bankrupt, decayed, decadent, and dangerous. So much for prophesy back in 1939.

Who would have prophesied that Richard Nixon, elected in 1968 as America's most durable and uncompromising anticommunist, would in just four years be embracing communists in China and calling for détente in Europe; that Mrs. Thatcher, victorious in privatizing the nation's economy, would, on her tenth anniversary as the Queen's first minister, have a public love affair with the Kremlin's chief communist commissar—just as Mr. Reagan left the White House cheerfully toasting the head of the Evil Empire?

Who would have thought that President François Mitterrand, elected in 1981 on a socialistic ticket and quickly nationalizing the big banks and everything else big, would, in only three years, recant, privatize, and travel to California to invite venture capitalists to open shop in France?

IBM not long ago had a world market share of ninety percent. Last year its R&D budget was near $6 billion (yes, billion), more than the entire sales of any of the world's other computer companies, save one. Though IBM still thrives, it now reels from the onslaught of obscure little computer companies in the United States and South Korea, some no longer so little or obscure. Who would have predicted only a decade ago that, all over the world, trade unions would become so quickly powerless and quiescent? Who would have predicted that in this era of affluence and rising expectations there would be this kinky nostalgia for the 1930s, a time of desperation, hopelessness, economic stagnation, fear, and anxiety; or that we would now have this bizarre skinhead adulation of Naziism?

Decades ago, to be modern, emancipated, and free meant being an apostle of reason, science, and scholarship. Today we have almost the exact opposite—thriving mysticism, the occult, astrology, tarot cards, incense, hallucinogens, Hare Krishna, Jesus cults, Hasidism, and Islamic fundamentalism, even among the better educated.

The West's lost generation of the 1920s, indifferent to anything but wine, poetry, jazz, and sex, became the aroused leftists of the 1930s. The autistic television kids of the 1950s, growing up coddled without a serious thought in their mutilated minds, became the sectarian rebels of the 1960s. And today they have become the anxious middle-class parents of kids everywhere tempted with samples of cocaine.

There are some trends without a future, and some futures not identified in the identifiable trends. Nor is this true just of social matters or among people who back in university days read history or literature or were otherwise innumerate.

The year 1953 was the fiftieth anniversary of the great Wright brothers' flight at Kitty Hawk, North Carolina, the first heavier-than-air motorized flight. So the *Aeronautical Engineering Review,* the premier journal of flight, did the obligatory thing: it published a fiftieth anniversary edition. Half was retrospective, with stories of biplanes and references to brave aviators in funny hats, goggles, leather jackets, and scarves. The other half was prospective—the next fifty years, written credibly by leading flight technocrats like Willie Lee and Wernher von Braun.

The prognostications contained nothing on the coming space age. The authors authoritatively foretold futures consisting entirely of winged atmospheric missiles, like the German buzz bombs with which some of the authors had a paternal familiarity. Four years later, in 1957, the space age erupted when Sputnik was propelled into orbit. The prognosticators became suddenly obsolete. Four years after that the *Aeronautical Engineering Review* itself became extinct.

In 1967 Herman Kahn and Tony Wiener published *The Year 2000,* about which Mr. Kahn made a lot of profitable speeches to groups of businessmen such as this one today, and did a lot of futurism research for companies such as also represented here today. The book became a mine of embarrassments: oil was mentioned only once—in a relaxed discussion of extraction from shale. Nothing about Islam or the Middle East. By the mid-1970s they expected fast-breeder reactors for nuclear power plants, providing cheap electricity and large amounts of desalinated water for coastal cities everywhere. There was nothing about the overcrowding of cities everywhere, slums, the underclass, the coming of Asia's new industrial tigers; nothing about the idea that Europe might actually get its economic act together, that the United Kingdom might abandon the left and Sweden shift from its famous Middle Way, or that the Soviet empire might rattle and lurch erratically to God-knows-where.

All this is prototypical of futurology. I will spare you recitation of the delicious embarrassments in *Future Shock* and *The Third Wave* and note only that *Megatrends 2000* tells us breathlessly about lots of familiar things, and tells us also that the big story of the 1990s will not be that of high tech but of the arts, literature, and spirituality, which will replace sports as the great leisure activity of the age. Cities will decline against the emergence of the quality-of-life rural area, facilitated by the new communications and information-based technologies. So certain are the authors of what will change that they simply ignore the rest, which will presumably remain forever fixed and firm—like the Warsaw Pact and other small matters in the general vicinity of the rest of the world.

Futurology is a beautiful profession. Its market is especially big among business people of high and important rank, the decision makers. The most important thing about decisions—indeed, the *only* thing to understand about decisions—is that they have futurity. They are not about the past, which is gone, done, and finished, or about the present, which is embedded and weighted down by existing conditions. They are only about the future. So, the higher your managerial rank, the more the future is your particular metier. You are therefore the futurologists' target audience, and targetted you get, shot at with rapid-fire projectiles of glowing possibilities that lie plausibly ahead. The only problems they foresee are glibly dismissed as easily solvable. By whom? You guessed it, by you, the people who do real work.

The professional futurist is invariably an extrapolator. Safely, his futures are plausible extrapolations of what is presently known, ratcheted lyrically upward into a new domain. He speaks only of things you've observed—telecommunications, computers, biogenetics, demographics, pop culture—clippings from the press. These are his building blocks, never anything you are not likely to have heard about. (Until a few months ago he had nothing to say about cold—really *warm*—fusion, about which, of course, there may be absolutely nothing to say.)

The futurist assumes that the future resides in the present, the present that you know. That is where he is so mistaken and irresponsibly misleading. The future also resides in the future itself, in tomorrow's present, and the many subsequent presents, one tomorrow after another, where in each succeeding year systems dynamics takes over to generate unpredictable futures and impossible predictabilities.

It is useful when speaking of what will happen to ask what else has to happen for the forecasted futures to happen. Consider again the suggestion that the networked home computer will liberate us from the curse of commuting, enabling us thus to live remotely in quiet rural removal. But will you really want all that quietude and isolation? Are you likely to want to stay home that much? Will your spouse want you there all the time? Will you really want all that many accidental children? What about the go-getters who continue to commute, who continue to make honest-to-goodness face-to-face sales calls?

It is impossible to know what will happen. Not everything that is possible is probable. Not everything that is desirable is doable. No wonder the Chinese aphorism says that forecasting is very difficult, especially with respect to the future.

Futurology is based on the attractive but utterly fallacious assumption that continuity of time (February follows January) is matched by a parallel continuity of events—a predictable linearity of man's fate.

Growth and genealogy are actual enough in the world of plants and animals. A child's physical development confirms the continuity of growth in time. It becomes an adult, like a little cabbage becoming bigger in time. But it requires a mighty metaphoric leap to make a symmetrical transference of the principle of biological growth and continuity in time to the social universe. In the social world we must not confuse change with time, or extrapolate events. If you'd extrapolated bustling London of 1880, jammed commercially with wagons and carriages, for fifty years, you would have come to the conclusion that by 1930 every square foot of London would be covered over with ten feet of horse manure.

Why did England turn out one way and Russia become such a mess? Why is Hungary so different? Why did England, Germany, and northern Italy get industrialized and not Spain? Why did Buenos Aires grow into such a beautiful and cosmopolitan metropolis and then regress into shabbiness without Beirut's excuse of religious or civil warfare? Why did Japan, a slim string of volcanic islands without natural resources or fertile land, located remotely from the world's modernity, and with an impenetrable language, and Singapore, equally remote and deeply impoverished—why did these two suddenly thrive, while far behind, with a greater population, a familiar Western language, and facilitating gifts of abundant natural resources, deep seaports, and a benign climate, located cheek-by-jowl next to the world's largest and richest single market, languishes Mexico?

Nothing is preordained—in nature, nations, or business. Humankind intervenes, not just to enhance or multiply, but also to constrain and detract. The future does not ascend linearly upward, no matter how upwardly rich its possibilities or optimistically rousing its advocates. Humankind makes its own future, and it is not guaranteed good.

The world is nonparametric. History does not move smoothly forward on perfectly parallel railroad tracks laid down by rational social engineers. Many things characterized as trends are merely incidents. They erupt in furious and visible activity, and then die. People speak of the changes they see so abundantly, but rarely do they note what has not changed, what abides. What so often they refer to as change lacks perspective—what they witness is activity, not certifiable change.

There are of course powerfully transforming changes that churn our times. They should be noted and understood. There is the shift from mechanical and electromechanical devices to electronics, from scale to miniaturization, the digitization of most things, the conversion of some people's knowledge into everybody's software, rapid accelerations in transport and communications, and fundamental new creations in genetic engineering, chemistry, inorganic materials, and knowledge itself.

All these shape what will be. We can specify some consequences, such as increased life expectancy, and something about what must ensue, such as the social carrying costs of aging. But we cannot name specific outcomes with any more confidence today than could London's futurists in 1880 or the distinguished physicist and member of the U.S. Atomic Energy Commission who, in 1955, envisioned a world where "a few generations hence, energy may be free—as free as unmetered air."

Those who launch enterprises to the specific prophesies of professional futurists, eminent scientists, or phrenologists are alike headed for trouble.

89

That is why I will not speak knowingly or in specific details about the future. Nor would I speak similarly about the great obligatory issues of the moment: 1992, Japan, *perestroika,* globalization, the changing work force, China after Tiananmen Square, the artificially intelligent Star Wars factory in the making, superconductivity, fusion, or seventeen other miracles before breakfast, and especially not about the world's chronic basket case, Africa. Africa is not a problem. It is a condition, characterized by a multiplicity of different problems. These cannot be rationally solved or imposed. They are too varied and complicated. Things will happen. Mathematicians solve mathematical problems, but other problems get resolved, not solved—finally worked out by time, conditions, forces, and by people who do real work.

In any case, the difficult part of problem-solving is anticipating the problems that the solutions create. The solution to a problem changes the problem. On the other hand, if you don't understand the problem, a successful solution is just an accident. Things are so complicated I find it convenient to identify with the college student of whom the professor asked, "The biggest problem we have in America today is ignorance and apathy, don't you agree Burns?" Burns answered, "I don't know and I don't care."

Consider our times. How can you make sense of a world in which all the forces of technology and commerce drive relentlessly towards globalization, where everywhere the world's wants and wishes press toward a converging commonality in consumption and in industrial and commercial systems—and yet where the precise opposite happens: polarization and parochialism, growing nationalism, regionalism, religious factionalism, and ethnic separatism? And in commerce itself there is increasing market fragmentation and microsegmentation. How can you make sense of all these contradictions and disjunctions?

With everything in such a seemingly chaotic and centrifugal whirl, what speaker would be brave or dumb enough to speak confidently in broad daylight about the future? What speaker would enter this rhetorical arena with words that many of you will dispute and that events will soon contradict? Not me.

Much better to stick to simple alleviating nostrums, such as that man does not live by bread alone, but principally by catchphrases. We have learned to live also by litigation. Recently in Chicago a psychic, having charged that a CAT scan destroyed her miraculous powers, successfully sued for a million dollars. God save us from justice and ourselves. Our national product has become gross, our landscape polluted by insatiably empty-headed critics who see diabolic connections everywhere and make distinctions nowhere. Give a little boy a hammer and he'll find lots of things that need pounding. Everybody seems a little boy, irresponsibly approaching everything with a completely open mouth.

Actually the situation, as Mark Twain said of Wagner's music, is not as bad as it sounds. Things are getting less worse. Materialism, selfishness, greed, envy—these are not in sudden new abundance. It is just that we've become more observant.

The world is actually in remarkably good condition. Peace breaks out everywhere, and now even Davidoff of Switzerland threatens to suspend cigar purchases from Castro's Cuba. Never before has the world been so compassionate; so full of communality and global civic-mindedness, with massive welfare and support programs for the poor, open immigration doors for the politically oppressed; so attuned to having and restoring a more livable physical environment, with medical care for all (voted into existence everywhere where people vote), with a huge and well-functioning World Health Organization, and with the International Monetary Fund to help out profligate nations who got themselves into trouble in the first place by arguing that the backwardness and poverty of other nations made them morally good credit risks. South Africa gets ever closer to getting into civilized line because of economic and other pressures from elsewhere. Nobody that cares about the opinions of others any longer separates what is good business from what is good citizenship.

Nor has it been television or takeovers that have corrupted the soul and dissipated the dream, especially in the West where these have been most abundant. It is well to remember what the dominant folk beliefs of the West tell us—that man lost his innocence not in the coruscating materialism of recent times but in a garden—the Garden of Eden. It was lost in paradise, not in Soho, on Forty-second Street, in Amsterdam, on the Ginza, or in the exotic pleasure palaces of Bangkok.

It is getting constantly clearer how best to run the world. First, keep the deep thinkers and heavy planners back in their stalls. Things that are left to chance get a lot better. What feels good is good only because it feels good. This has nothing to do with whether it really is good. The more people say something is good today, the worse they are likely to feel about it tomorrow. In the world of human affairs, nothing is predetermined until after it has happened, no matter how elegant the theory.

In the world of my principal habitation, the university, a really good thing is to have a good theory. If the theory doesn't work in practice, we are convinced there is something wrong with practice. In some circles, after all is said and done, mostly all that's done is said.

The world is inherently unstable because it is populated by people with will, energy, and imagination. They do things. They won't leave well enough alone. That is why success is only a transient condition, not a result. Nothing is ever finished or fixed, not even in the paradise of which we just spoke. Adam said to Eve upon their expulsion from the Garden of Eden, "This, my dear, is a time of transition." It always is.

Woody Allen said that ninety percent of success is just showing up, which I interpret to mean being attentive and aware, being alive and sensibly responsive to what is happening. This is different from listening uncritically to commercial prognosticators of what will happen. That is not an effective way to live.

In any case, you live only once. If you do it right, once is enough. The trick is to make of it something sensible, noble, profitable, and fun—in short, a good thing, of which that late great piano-playing sybarite, Liberace, said that too much of a good thing is just the right amount. He was not a modest man. I once knew a man so modest and considerate of others that when asked what two plus two equaled he said, "Four, but I could be wrong."

As you can imagine, he was not one of the world's great master builders. The race may not always be to the swift, nor the battle to the strong, but that is the way to bet. Surely that is so in this age of fast history, of rapid acceleration. It is not so much the accurately forecasted future we

93

need as attentiveness and quick response to the forces that are shaping today's events and environment.

I have mentioned some of these. They are clear and persistent enough. But they did not descend upon us suddenly without warning like a thunderclap on a clear day. There are always indicators. *Natura non facit saltum,* wrote Alfred Marshall, the father of microeconomics. Nature does not take leaps. Much changes, but more abides. Things change rapidly, but not often instantaneously. The most pervasively transforming instrument of our times, the computer, is, after all, over fifty years old. Things happen suddenly only to people who have been inattentive. That is why prophecy is less important than attentiveness and agility.

Regarding the future where, indeed, we will have to spend the rest of our lives, the necessity for action cannot be avoided by flight into rhetoric or isolation into analysis. We must get organized for action. Study, calculation, and budgeting reduce uncertainty and transform it into risk. We may have to study and calculate faster, but also with more reliance on the common sense that nature, wisdom, and experience confer. Experience comes from what we have done, wisdom from what we have done badly.

In an age of fast history, you need the agility of the gazelle to get things done and the stability of the elephant to keep from getting knocked over by what others have done. Agility requires courage, and you'd be surprised how much easier it is to be courageous when you're big and strong and have deep pockets.

The world is run mostly by emotion and justified by calculation. The future of your enterprise depends largely on the interplay between invention and vision, between technological capability and entrepreneurial quest, between the social dream and the organizational system in which the dream resides.

More than ever before, managerial effectiveness requires inspiration and shrewdness, fast decisions and firm decisiveness, courage linked to conviction, and, above all, the will to act. Increasingly it is more important to act fast than to think correctly about tomorrow, because what one must act on is what is already in the process of happening, not what might happen later. In the age of fast history, equivocation is more harmful than prediction is helpful.

So . . . things are little different than when God told Noah to build an ark so that he, his family, and all the species of the earth could survive the flood he'd let loose in two weeks. Shocked, Noah said, "Two weeks? God, do you know how long it takes to build an ark?" And God replied, "Noah, how long can you tread water?" It got done in two weeks.

THREE

Operating

19

The Chryslerization
of America

ACTUALLY IT HAPPENED first at Lockheed in 1971, but most
memorably and spectacularly at Chrysler in 1980, when
finally, hat in hand, Chrysler went to Washington.

Asked in Ernest Hemingway's *The Sun Also Rises* how
he went bankrupt, Mike Campbell replied, "Two ways.
Gradually and then suddenly." At Chrysler things disas-
sembled for years under managements whose shoelaces
seemed permanently untied. Then, suddenly, it was Mike
Campbelled.

Chrysler's misfortunes were widely blamed on the vil-
lainous Japanese. But imports hurt Chrysler largely because it was already deeply crippled, uncompetitive in a
tenaciously uncompetitive domestic industry.

With the outlook grimmer by the day, new management, playing hardball, renegotiated and restructured everything. Washington became the lender and guarantor of last resort, settling for what are now called junk bonds, complete with an equity kicker.

Eventually, Chrysler emerged from purgatory precisely because it chose purgatory rather than immediate immolation in bankruptcy. In purgatory the new management cleansed, slimmed, and renewed the company.

In the late 1980s there began a massive Chryslerization of America—a continuing purge of companies complete with draconian restructurings, dismemberments, revised philosophies and practices, and, of course, junk bonds (which, of course, they were not). As with Chrysler, emphasis began to be on focus, clarity, agility, vigor, action, lean staffs, and on simple, direct management styles—back to basics.

The new round of Chryslerization had its own villain— Mr. T. Boone Pickens, the founding godfather remembered best for his daring run on Gulf Oil. Waves of imitators quickly followed. With packs of lawyers and investment bankers prowling everywhere for vulnerable prey, some companies Chryslerized themselves defensively to avoid victimization. In one three-week period in 1986 alone, Transworld Corporation, Holiday Corporation, and United Technologies, each on the face quite healthy companies, announced massive unforced restructurings. Each clearly thought itself entirely too appetizing a meal for predators attracted to the taste of fat.

The Chryslerization of America has been deeply systemic, and it will continue. Pickens was only the messenger. It occurs everywhere in all industries, unstopped and unstoppable by changes in tax laws, acrobatic anti-takeover

100

tactics, or the incarceration of white-collar hooligans. On the surface, it looks unrelated to Chrysler's troubles with the Japanese—but of course that's wrong. Everything is related to the new global competition, even a restructuring as seemingly remote as that of the Kroger Company supermarket chain.

The globalization of competition explains almost everything. It represents the end of sheltered domestic insularity, the rise of agile new competitors from distant places who've not been conditioned to the easy accommodations of a fat society. That is why the Pickens round of Chryslerizations has been only the beginning of events that can be properly characterized as deep transformation. Takeovers and restructurings will surely continue for a long time. And they know no boundaries of geography or company size. European companies are in the same throes—and even the bigger and older Japanese companies. Nippon Steel has announced plant closings, a major reorganization, and reductions in force. Everybody is now vulnerable to distant competitors. Everybody has to get leaner and better.

Whatever else may be said, the Chryslerization of America and especially of corporatedom in the rest of the West will make the respective national economies healthier and more vigorous, as Chrysler itself finally became—and surprisingly fast. Unfortunately, in purgatory things seem painfully long, with emphasis on the pain.

Some speak ominously about the pain of other consequences—that all this forces management into a dangerously obsessive concentration on the short term, on producing cash today rather than building seriously for tomorrow. Perhaps so, but that presumes an unlikely linearity. People and institutions seldom foul their own nests

101

for long, in part because events and conditions force them back to their senses.

Meanwhile much falseness gets solemnly said. Chryslerization is inherently unpopular. Nobody likes being a victim—of downsizing, early retirement, or anything else. Everybody who might be victimized is therefore powerfully attracted to the notion that what's bad for somebody is bad for everybody, now and in the future. For those especially disposed to lofty cerebration, posterity suddenly gets solicitous attention. The attack on the status quo is given a bad social name.

The future comes from the present, but it occurs in the future. Neither people nor institutions are bound inflexibly or forever to the conditions from which they emerge. That explains progress. People will generally find a way to do what they really want and need to do. Posterity is not in jeopardy.

20

The Pluralization
of Consumption

THE END OF mass markets and mass marketing is constantly proclaimed. Evidence is suggested by the growing proliferation of products and brands in all categories, the miniaturization of segments and sectors, and the multiplication of small market niches.

It would be a terrible mistake to believe this simple message, and disastrous to act upon it.

Things are not what they seem. The earth is not centrifugal, stationary, flat, or chaotic. It spins on its axis, rotates in an elliptical orbit, and regularly unleashes a bewildering and largely unpredictable variety of weathers and catastrophes. Markets are also not what they seem, though they seem suddenly proliferating and disorderly. A Copernican view suggests another interpretation to which no business can afford to be inattentive.

Every corner of the globe now gets increasingly subjected to similar communications—commercial, cultural, social, and hard-news. Consciousness converge towards modernity and global commonality. Preferences get cosmopolized and consumption homogenized.

Yet, perversely, heterogeneity and parochialism thrive—religious dogmatism, raging nationalism, escalating ethnicity. And markets fragment, even within nations. Dozens of detergent items congest the stores, automotive multiplicities clog the roads, and propagation accelerates in personal computers, engineering workstations, toiletries, TV transmission, convenience foods, cameras, financial services, health care, ready-to-eat cereals, apparel, soft drinks, machine tools, chemicals, airlines, magazines, polymers, jeans, retailing institutions, and on and on.

The more powerfully homogenizing and relentlessly globalized the world's communications and commerce get, the more varied its products and more numerous its consuming segments seem to become. The world suddenly looks remarkably Hegelian, even centrifugal.

But it would be wrong to characterize what we see as fragmentation or proliferation, or to view the persistence of inherited local, national, and ethnic consuming preferences as contradicting the theory of global homogenization.

What changes does not disconfirm what endures. Absence of evidence is not evidence of absence. At some stage, established mass markets usually divide into lots of small specialty ones, except that now this happens sooner and faster, and all the new segments show up everywhere.

The global boom in ethnic food specialties is a microcosm of what's happening in all product categories. Suddenly, in the world's urban places the demand thrives for ethnic fast foods: pizza, hamburgers, sushi, frankfurters, Greek salad, Chinese egg rolls, pita bread, croissants, tapas, curry, bagels, chili, doughnuts, french fries, and even Sacher torte. Everybody who can get them wants them, regardless of national residence, origin, religion, tradition, or even taboos. Suddenly everybody everywhere simultaneously occupies each of these product-market segments—often several on a given day, even at a given eating occasion.

In all product categories and places, people increasingly occupy many and often disparate segments, and circulate among varied brands. Customer segments are no longer tightly discrete or distinct. Segments have become porous and coincident. Customers are now segment migrants, with multiple segment preferences at the same time. They've become heteroconsumers, as in a cafeteria, making seemingly idiosyncratic choices. This is as true of high-tech as of high-touch products and as true of industrial and commercial consumers as of household consumers.

Yet there's a converging rationality. Consider again the scrambled variety of ethnic food preferences. What people want is not just the variety of these foods, but their convenient, fast, low-cost, and nutritious availability. In that sense, everybody is in the same single segment, a segment that consists of people with plural preferences satisfiable in a similar convenient fashion.

In this new world of segment simultaneity and pluralization of consumption, it would be a bad mistake for a company to treat the heteroconsumer as if he or she were the
occupant of a fixed and narrow segment. Most companies
offer relatively wide lines of products, sizes, features, and
forms in a given category. But mostly they do this for what
have become the wrong reasons. The old right reasons were
to have a line of items suitable specifically for each large,
distinctive, and definable preference group. The new right
reasons should be to have what serves and attracts people
who've become increasingly alike and indistinct from one
another, and yet have simultaneously varied and multiple
preferences.

It would therefore also be a bad mistake to advertise a
product or service as if the intended audience remained
monolithic and singular, characterized demographically,
psychologically, or functionally by a fixed structure of
wants and wishes. This is no longer how things are, and it
poses one of marketing's major creative challenges.

The challenge is global. The rapid acceleration of cheap
and easy communication, transport, and travel globalizes
competition and cosmopolizes consumption. The world's
consumption preferences are driven simultaneously toward
both standardization and pluralization—standardization in
the sense that these preferences now appear everywhere,
and pluralization in the sense that everywhere people want
the same variety—in the stores, at home, in factories,
fields, mines, offices, laboratories, schools, temples; regarding the sacred and the secular, work and play, study
and diversion, reality and fantasy.

Nothing is exempt from the allure of new possibilities—
for personal expression and fulfillment, for lightening work

and enhancing life. Everybody is attracted to the multiple possibilities of modernity, including, coincidentally and paradoxically, the preservation of deeply remembered traditions and loyalties. These are deeply remembered and strongly coveted precisely because so much modernity is so alluring and unsettling. That helps explain the global eruptions of nationalistic, ethnic, and religious intensities. Humankind, said T. S. Eliot, cannot stand too much change or reality. It needs roots, remembrance, attachments, fantasy, and transcendence, while wanting simultaneously everything else that beckons within palpable reach.

Possibilities expand for people to have exactly what they wish, and at mass-produced prices—prices that are low not so much because of improved or flexible manufacturing but rather because of global scale economies. The kinds of small market segments common in Switzerland now appear also in Sri Lanka and Swaziland. Everywhere people learn from the same communal messenger, while prices descend into increasingly attractive reach. Additively, similar small preferences in many places cumulate into global bigness in all places. No product category—consumer or industrial, tangible or intangible, consumable or durable—is exempt.

All products everywhere undergo the division of monolithic big segments into porous little ones. Though consumption thus gets pluralized and miniaturized, its global aggregate gets magnified. The competitive possibilities for scale and scope become compelling. Those who act on these possibilities capture economizing advantages, to the envy and regret of those who only sit and wait.

Few firms can escape the churn of necessities imposed by intensified global competition. Almost all companies will have to widen their geographic reach and offerings. Even

107

those that choose to specialize geographically, or tightly in a narrow line, will have to operate globally. That is the only way to capture the scale economies necessary to get and keep costs down, get access to low-cost suppliers, and generate sufficient cash to finance the development and innovations that competitiveness requires.

Success therefore becomes a matter of combining global reach with local vigor, and of developing new, efficient ways to address and serve the public that is so ambidextrously engaged in heteroconsumption.

21

Customers, Money, and Conscience

A BUSINESS IS about only two things—money and customers. It takes money to get started, customers to keep going, and more money to hold on to existing customers and attract new ones. Hence the two central activities of every business are marketing and finance.

Finance deals with the acquisition, management, and control of money, activities that are always strained and competitive. You get money by competing for it, dispense money among contenders for it, and control money by overseeing its use by people who'd rather be left alone.

Marketing gets customers by inducing them to switch from competitors, keeps customers by staying better than competitors, and creates entirely new customers by offering things of such irresistibility that they shatter people's natural inertia, indifference, or active sales resistance.

The amount of capital a company needs depends on the intensity of the competition it faces and on the nature, pace, and acceleration of its industry. The greater the acceleration, the more capital is needed to keep up, let alone get ahead of all the others who are trying to get ahead. Any lapse in a company's ability to generate capital for itself produces an almost instant deterioration of its competitive capability and spirit.

When capital gets short or beyond easy reach, this lack quickly creates constraints. It generates resistance and a grudging attitude toward spending money for things that are not instantly self-justifying, especially innovation, experimentation, R&D, organizational development, new equipment to replace the still-working old, and hiring and nurturing the people on whose enterprise and initiative the future of the enterprise depends.

Nothing distorts possibilities and inhibits enterprise so much as the absence of funds necessary for enterprise. It is almost impossible for a company to have too much money, to have more than it can use to help shape its own thriving future. This does not mean it should have a cash-rich balance sheet or be indifferent to economy, only that it should have such an abundance of capital, or such reliable access to it, as to feel easily comfortable about doing what ought to be done.

All this means that everybody, whether responsible for the whole business or some small part of it, should constantly consider the financial and customer-getting consequences of everything—of what's being done, contemplated, and not done. If something doesn't pass one or preferably both these tests, something is wrong. It calls for action—and now, not later.

It is therefore the obligation of every manager, regardless of the level or reach of his or her responsibilities, constantly to assert and impose these tests, and to take appropriate actions. Little else matters by comparison . . . except one thing.

It matters how people feel about the moral legitimacy and social worth of what they do, and about the people with whom they are associated. The world's work is not naturally noble. Its outcomes are not automatically symmetrical or benign. To force all business decision-making and actions into the fixed mold of customer and financial considerations imposes a harsh and narrow discipline. It is a necessary and compelling discipline, but never sufficient and often nasty. Standing alone, ungoverned by higher values and commands, it can and usually does become grotesque.

One supposes that people who lead and manage are, like everybody else, kept in balance by a moral gyroscope of sorts, some ethical standards, some sense of social duty and decency, some guiding principles of right and wrong; that they are possessed of some character, conscience, and even nobility. Without these, nothing else is worth saying or prescribing.

22

Making Sense About
Strategy and Customers

FEW THINGS CHARACTERIZE modern management so much
as the escalating stream of constantly varying advice about
how to improve performance. Remarkably, most of this
advice is silent about the one big thing that counts most.

Consider strategy. One fashionable orthodoxy follows
another, each asserting a superior merit over the other.
Look only at the list: planning, long-range planning, strategic planning, portfolio strategy, PIMS, the experience
curve, management by objectives, excellence, competitive
analysis, competitive advantage, the focused factory, flexible manufacturing, competing through service, competing

on quality, competing via information, and, most recently, strategic intent and competing on time. Around the edges are related suggestions: innovativeness, self-managed teams, entrepreneurship, design for manufacturability, service guarantees, flattening the organization, and now restructuring, which is partly about decentralization and defattening, partly about focus, and mostly about the promised instant enhancement of stockholder value.

How curious that so seldom is heard an encouraging word about customers and marketing.

In the end—really, at the outset—every activity or purpose underlying these labels is about getting and keeping customers. No matter what fashion or idea comes or goes, the one absolutely essential and therefore inescapable thing that must be done, and to which attention therefore always returns, is marketing. That is why marketing is always getting rediscovered. Even the infamous "takeover artists" and LBOers have their eyes firmly on the cash flows that can originate only from willing customers.

With marketing so central, why is it so peculiarly absent from most strategy concepts?

In fact it is not absent at all. It is just not spoken of, only assumed, like breathing, about which the doctor also says nothing unless you have emphysema. But merely assuming the necessity of marketing in a business does not assure that it is effectively there. In most companies it is mostly not. That is why it has to be so regularly resurrected, and usually with somber seriousness, by top management.

When attention slackens, as attention invariably does in general, things go bad. When bad enough, or not good enough, management returns to first principles—getting and keeping customers. Even policies that set out strategically to milk a product—to turn it into a cash cow—try to maximize and prolong the yield at some acceptable level of customer-keeping costs.

Because all business strategies are tightly dependent on customers, it makes sense to be explicit about what it takes to attract and hold them. Thus if strategies regarding product and service quality are about anything, they are about certain assessments of what's necessary to get and keep customers: quality is important, but quality of what kind, at what level, relative to what price, and with regard to which competitors? The same is true of the hidden assumptions regarding "competing on time," which is all about faster market responses and reducing cycle costs. What does it really mean? Lower costs to raise margins? Or reduce prices in order to raise, regenerate, or retain sales? Is that the theory: satisfy customers better by responding faster, and then also by getting costs down so that prices can get more competitive?

All strategies operate on certain implicit assumptions about what it takes to get and keep customers. Failing to speak explicitly about one's marketing assumptions is like expecting love to thrive without ever speaking the language of love.

A strategy that doesn't speak explicitly about customers and the competitive environment will surely fail to generate and sustain a proper level of customer and competitive consciousness in your company, especially in the important nooks and crannies where the real work gets done. People will speak with technocratic simplicity about doing certain specific things, but without regard to why and for whom. "Quality" will become an imposed dictum rather than an understood dedication; "fast response" a mechanical met-

114

ric rather than a meaningful motivation; "market share" a warlike target rather than an earned result; "self-managed teams" a comfortable indulgence rather than a purposefulness construct; "entrepreneurship" an escape from discipline rather than a leap into enterprise; "restructuring" a game of finance rather than a fight for market effectiveness. Employees get turned into tin soldiers, obediently taking orders to turn left or right without knowing right from wrong. With a tin ear they'll not hear the voice of the customer. Not being constructed to last, things will wind down. Entropy will triumph.

Finally, in extremis, marketing will get rediscovered—except that hardly anybody will remember how to do it, let alone what it is. Starting over becomes a long and dangerous voyage. Of course, to start over is better than to have gone under. The company probably kept going only because its competitors were taking the same bad advice for just as long. The falling tide, which lowered all ships, put none at a disadvantage, though some shattered on the shoals.

When it takes so little to keep the ship's crew focused always on its authentic purposes, why not avoid the rocky coastline in the first place?

23

Business-to-Business
Business

THE BUYING BEHAVIOR of businesses is heavily emotional, more so even than a consumer buying cosmetics in a retail store.

A woman shopping for makeup knows exactly what she's doing. She's trying to solve a problem, perhaps even to realize her fantasized intentions. She knows the product's limitations and applies a massive discount to the producer's alluring promises. No such self-knowledge attends industrial purchasing, where buyers think falsely of themselves as engaged in rational calculation about objective matters, as being professionally involved in serious matters of adult reasoning and negotiation. Business buyers who are in this way deluded by their own presumptions are especially vulnerable to being flummoxed by those who sell to them.

By and large businesses buy from other businesses via sales representatives, almost certainly when the sale involves high-ticket products, industrial or commercial systems, services, and commitments that are expected to last over some extended period of time. Purchasing decisions usually take a good while, involving a great deal of technical discussion, much passing of papers, and a lot of redesign and recalculation along the way.

Often it is not totally clear who is seller and who buyer— as, for example, a proposed joint venture or alliance regarding a new process control system for a chemical plant, when those who own the plant have as much to gain from the lead time of being its first user as those who design and manufacture the system have to gain from being able to use the plant as a beta site.

People meet over and over again, paper gets mailed and faxed, telephone voices confer, meals get consumed, sporting games get played and attended. Information is in these ways exchanged, processed, and assessed. In the end a purchase-and-sale agreement is reached. It is always believed and commonly asserted that the decision was indeed a "purchasing" decision (after all, it *was* a purchase, wasn't it?) and that somebody "decided" (after all, *didn't* somebody decide?). But of course decisions of this kind do not so much specifically get made as emerge. And of course the "seller" makes a "decision" too, though it is seldom specifically acknowledged. The "decision" is to accept the deal that's been hammered out and to acknowledge the other party to it.

117

The "other party" is called the buyer, who refers to the product and/or service specifications and financial terms as the basis for a "decision." But everybody knows that this is a convenient simplification. What really mattered was whether all that was said and promised was believable, whether things were as technically feasible and performance was as reasonably possible as promised—that is, whether the "seller", the source of the promises, was reliable and trustworthy and whether the "buyer" had the ability and intention to pay.

Even the most attractive specifications will be hobbled if installation services are suspected to be weak, applications help unreliable, parts and postpurchase services weak. To know in advance we look at the sellers' history and reputation and give them a thorough workover in discussions designed to clarify expectations and promises and test the suppliers' capabilities and commitments. We look their representatives straight in the eye over lunch and at some other preferably convivial and therefore unguarded moments.

All this helps explain some of the fixed rules of Thomas Watson, the elder, founder of IBM, whose salesmen were required always to wear fresh white shirts, dark suits, regimental ties, and hats, and never to drink when with the customer.

Of course, tangible products can be, and usually are, presented (that is, "sold") in ways other than their technical specifications alone. And this is true also of the literal descriptions of intangible industrial and commercial products (commonly called services). We need only note the exquisite care taken on the design and content of catalogs and brochures, on the attention lavished on the form in which proposals, specifications, and descriptions are presented. Neatness, facilitating graphics, clear and simple prose, right and varied typefaces, appropriate and often almost luxurious binders, audiovisual aids—all these are much attended to. Desktop printing thrives, largely to make more impressive and effective presentations to the impressionable people whom we seek to influence toward our custom.

The same is increasingly true of the external design of the most complex and sophisticated industrial products. Products must look at least as good as they claim to be, even better, just like people, who dress themselves not really to "bring out their best," but to suggest something better than what they privately know is actually there. This is a big departure from the times when locomotives looked like weird insects, with all the works on the outside.

The same principles of suggestiveness apply regarding the control panels of technologically complex and sophisticated machinery. They must be neat, easily readable, reachable, and useable, technicolored, with modern signalling alarms or automatic shutoffs. It is not enough for them merely to be right or functional. They must look right and state-of-the art, even if the guts are not.

Tests conducted on highly trained and responsible engineers and scientists in industrial purchasing situations repeatedly confirm that they are strongly suggestible regarding the external design appearances of products. The better these look by some nonfunctional standard, the better their functionality and reliability are judged to be. Furthermore, products and services are judged in important part by the appearance, manner, and presentations of sales engineers.

Clothes may not make the man, but they can help make the sale.

There is, of course, nothing especially new or unexpected about all this. But it is well to understand what is going on. The seller must be presumed to be technically on par with and economically "in the ballpark" of his competitors. That, as in poker, is the price of entry. But "presumed" is seldom determined by technical tests or comparisons. Rather, what is presumed is a combination of what is known about the thing promised and what is believed about the promisor.

Who wins in this game of poker is a matter of how the game is played. In the game, no matter how informed and experienced the buyer, no matter how technical, sophisticated, high-priced the product, or how specialized, arcane, important the service, winning is mostly a matter of the interplay of psychology and strategy. Though the winner is presumably chosen by the buyer, in the game itself the winner is susceptible to the same kinds of personal and emotional influences as when at home watching television advertisements for hair sprays, colognes, jeans, and beer.

There is only nominal difference between these two situations. To say the difference is real is equivalent to saying that a person is only shape or stature; the look instead of the being; appearance instead of essence.

The only reality that counts, assuming normal health and capability, is the inner self. All the rest is merely physiology. It is the inner self that decides all things, regardless of age, gender, education, or affiliation, whether at home, play, work, or in service. Order is the unending object of humanity's constant struggle between the mind and the brain.

120

Trust is even more important in commercial transactions than it is in the decisions of independent household consumers. Seldom does a commercial vendor have a patent monopoly on anything, and then not for long. Usually there is more than one source, so the choice depends largely on other matters, on claims, promises, and impressions that are not verifiable in advance. You have to go by what you've heard and experienced, and by your instincts. What makes trust especially important in the selection of a vendor is that unwanted and unexpected consequences of underperformance can be so terrible.

True, a shampoo that causes instant and irreversible baldness is unwanted and awful—perhaps worse than steel girders that collapse, memory chips that get permanent amnesia, a bank that suddenly withdraws its credit line. But the leverage of things gone wrong tends to be bigger regarding industrial and commercial purchases. The negative consequences of exaggerated, false, or stretched promises regarding the generic products involved in business-to-business transactions can have suddenly proliferating and uncorrectable effects that can ruin companies, lives, and careers. Mostly such incidents are rare.

The likelihood of promises getting violated is greater in purchasing of services than tangible products. It is especially high regarding the services and supply conditions that are packaged along with tangible products. This is because design, quality, and delivery are less easily or reliably controlled in services than in goods produced under close supervision inside the factory. Details are overlooked or forgotten. Deliveries get delayed, application support turns sloppy, emergency repair is late, billing is botched, inquiries are mishandled, account managers turn unresponsive, product enhancement falls behind. And all these are in addition to concern about the reliability and consistency of the generic product itself.

(It is an important mark of our new times that many former services are now technologized as tangible products. Perhaps the oldest modern example is musical recordings, followed by motion pictures, and then plastic credit cards. The current most powerful and pervasive example is computer software. All four replace live and idiosyncratically performing professionals with reliable and consistent industrialized services made in the factory.)

In a tightly integrated and closely scheduled industrial and commercial society, the many possibilities for failure in the quality and delivery of services raise the consciousness and apprehensions of negotiators. One should therefore not be surprised that emotional factors are uniquely and deeply present in the purchasing behavior of business people, especially in industrial firms. Reminders are frequent of how fast even strong and gigantic firms can suddenly implode due to a single or a related series of contaminating or failed events. One quickly sees why trust is so important, why in so many large and small ways it is constantly sought, cultivated, tested, and influenced in business relationships.

Of course the importance of trust and reputation has always been widely noted among people of affairs. Words need not be spoken to attest to their centrality or prevalence. Indeed, they have become so important that the old declaration "My word is my bond" has become somewhat suspect. It should not have to be said. These days it is uttered mostly by the con artist at the county fair—obsolete and discredited cant, designed to violate the very trust that it seeks.

Trust and reputation are not discretionary. They have always been necessary for doing business, and increasingly so as those who deal with each other are strangers and live distantly from each other. They are as necessary in business as the people in whom they reside.

In no way is this more obvious than in the many activities and elaborate rituals that characterize the relations between business buyer and business seller. Often they appear casually social, convivially involving play, food, drink, and spouses. In fact they are anything but casual. The rituals are fixed and taken seriously by their participants. Their purposes are clear but unspoken—to test one another's veracity, reliability, and trustworthiness, to create and reciprocate obligations of performance, and to ascertain via close observance in casual settings the extent to which claims and promises that cannot be tested in advance can be relied upon, lest terrible consequences follow later.

The better the seller's reputation, the more believable are the company representatives. The more believable the representatives, the better is the seller's reputation. And so the easier it becomes to select that seller from among all others. In this sense sales representatives are also perambulating advertising media for their company, trying to build and enhance its customer-getting and customer-keeping reputation. Few things are so reliably true and understandably reliable as things whose truths are attested by their venerability.

24

Cost Evasions and Gross Margin Escapes

COSTS ARE ALWAYS higher than expected, even when they are expected to fall. They require scrupulous scrutiny and constant containment.

Costs naturally rise because natural commercial forces and inclinations move irrepressibly in that direction. Suppliers push them up to the limit at which they can keep old customers and still attract new ones. Labor wants wages, benefits, and amenities kept up, and usually resists short-term job-eliminating cost reductions. Customers in the channels of distribution (the trade), feeling their oats, want vendors to bear more delivery and warehousing costs while simultaneously wanting payment for trade information on

124

stock movements, for advertising, and for access to preferred positions at retail.

Costs have the same natural tendency to rise as rocks have to fall. They also have a natural tendency to be denied and to resist being accounted for: "I didn't incur and can't control them. They were here before I was. Anyhow, they're overhead."

Resistance and refusal are especially prevalent under conditions of joint production—when more than one product is produced simultaneously with others in the same place, and when there are other common or joint costs, such as for occupancy, administration, distribution, and the like. Rather than hassle about allocation formulas, it becomes attractive simply to eliminate the necessity of making allocations at all. The usual way consists of an inspired creation, a fictitious accounting category that resides quietly far away someplace else. To it inconvenient and contestable costs can be handily assigned without their drawing serious scrutiny or anybody's coming to identify them. It is called "overhead"—operating overhead, capital overhead, corporate overhead, common overhead, just so long as it is remote and "not mine."

There is a generally agreed rationale for this fiction. It is to stop the bickering about allocation and "get on with the job." The only problem is that the job suffers from nobody's being held responsible for costs that get incurred but are not charged to anybody.

Denial and evasion are also common with new products, especially more sophisticated new ones with heavy introductory selling costs. While heavy launch costs are usually expected in advance, they are almost chronically underesti-

mated, as everyone knows from experience but keeps repeating in practices.

The reasons are fairly obvious. New products have high
selling costs because they require channels and final customers to change their minds, to agree to switch from
existing products, practices, and behavior. Persuading
them to change is rarely cheap. The more sophisticated the
new product and the more it departs in various ways from
the familiar and accustomed (say, from electromechanical
to electronic, from metal to plastic, from distributed processing to workstations), the greater will be its direct selling
cost, the costs of field-training and customer education and
support, and the like. The customer's decision-making
process will be more deliberative, more cumbersome, and
slower. It will take longer to get the application on stream
after it is actually bought, and longer to operate smoothly.

There are reasons why the anticipated high costs of all
these are usually underestimated. For one thing, there is
Murphy's famous law: If anything can go wrong, it will.
And so it does. Anybody who knows anything knows that
things rarely go smoother and faster than expected. This
brings us to a second reason.

Systematic biases lurk in all new-product activities—
underestimation of development and introduction times
and costs, and overestimation of consumer receptiveness
and revenues. Expectations are always euphoric, at least
when they are out in the open. Though people try to be
realistic in estimating what it will take to make a new
product succeed, and they build higher gross margins into
its price to cover higher selling costs (to say nothing of the
costs of development), once they commit themselves they
also commit to the product's success. Belief in success

requires belief—a positive attitude. Unfortunately, this tends to distort everything in a favorable direction. And it generates impatience with agnostics whose realism gets in the way. They will be seen as having negative attitudes. Thus realism retreats before the momentum of the believers. Later all tasks will turn out to be more difficult and take longer than the believers budgeted for. Most especially the marketing launch will be more difficult, slower, and more costly than originally estimated.

It is a mistake in this context to think of gross margins in the conventional way. In fact, the conventional way may itself be mistaken. When selling costs are especially high, and deeply integral to a product's success, it becomes especially sensible to factor them into the product's direct costs at the outset rather than leave them hanging residually to be covered later by "higher-than-normal" gross margins. Acknowledging these likely costs in advance leads to more realistic and disciplined practices later. It also acknowledges that they are not discretionary, which they are not. When costs are real and unavoidable, it is hard to see the point of ignoring them in the original bookkeeping.

It will be said that they are not ignored because they appear at the outset in the business plan that deals with the cost of the launch. But that is precisely the point. Treating them separately as "cost of the launch" gets the bookkeeping entirely wrong. They are not separate costs, but a cost of the product itself. They are deeply integral to the product, never avoidable, and rarely discretionary. In absence of the special efforts and costs of its launch, the product would have no more commercial existence than if one of its critical features were similarly absent. A product that people don't buy is not a product. It's an artifact, like in a museum. Realism dictates that the bookkeeping treat the product's launch costs as core development costs and that they be entered right along with its other obvious costs that must be accounted for before accounting for the gross margin.

Some companies use the terms gross margin and gross profit interchangeably. That is self-deluding and possibly self-immolating. It allows people to get accustomed to thinking of something as being "profit" when clearly identifiable and continuing costs yet remain to be paid for. It gets people thinking complacently about unattainable heights of profitability when they should be feeling a compelling urgency about exactly what needs doing in order to have any kind of profit at all.

And it is confusing. Gross margin is not by any definitional acrobatics the same as gross profit. A margin refers to an amount or proportion available to help cover unstated costs and contributions to profit. We know that certain unstated but definable costs are there. One reason for having left them unstated is the difficulty of their exact quantitative attribution to specific products, departments, functions, or time periods. They get buried in one of those ubiquitous overhead categories.

As we have noted, difficulties of cost attribution and allocation are avoided by resort to an accounting fabrication into which, by common consensus, they can be legitimately dumped. This is convenient, congenial, and highly addictive. It avoids the labor of calculation, the discipline of tight controls, and the discomfort of colleagues who would otherwise be pitted against each other in mutual efforts to minimize their own targeting.

It is often said that it is cheaper and more efficient to avoid struggle than to compel an artificial and always contentious accountability. On the other hand, nothing so much contaminates practice and distorts judgment as denial of uncongenial realities and evasion of unpleasant duties. Nobody likes to pay for costs when avoidance is possible via an easy accounting artifact. Nobody likes fighting over allocation formulas when it is so simple and agreeable to allow undistributed costs to pile up distantly in general overhead.

These evasions alone are good arguments in favor of full-absorption costing. Avoiding problems of joint-allocation and full-absorption costing does not avoid incurring the costs. Worse, it incurs problems of pricing and profit measurement. You cannot know what, minimally, are the prices at which you can afford to sell if you do not know what your fully absorbed costs are.

It is in the nature of the vertically integrated and the decentralized organization, and of the division of labor in operations, that people, departments, subsidiaries, and divisions will deny and shirk responsibility for any costs not directly and unambiguously attributable to them. All incentives are to deny them and to deny their allocability in a fair way. The usual result is that a big pool of unabsorbed costs sloshes loosely around in the corporation, left irresponsibly to be covered somehow and, in the end, corporately, where nobody is accountable. Where nobody is accountable nobody is responsible. Nobody with real responsibilities benefits from trying to contain or eliminate the costs that slosh around in this pool. Anybody who tries only gets hassles.

This malignancy never stops by itself. It metastasizes. In the operating organization where the real work of organizations gets done, there is both the incentive and the possibility to control and reduce costs. Full-absorption costing eliminates the pool. All corporate services are paid for, corporate capital is paid for, period costs are accounted and paid for. Everything.

Mostly, introduction of this system will be resisted. Since all costs must be directly accounted for, for every part of the organization there will be some new charges, some pain. The only possibilities of gain are in comparison with the organization's other operating divisions, departments, companies, product lines. Since everybody will want, at least in self-defense, to gain, the probability of reciprocal pain for everybody else is high. Though everybody will scramble for a system that minimizes absorptions, everybody will become deeply cost conscious and actively cost-containing.

In this respect, organizational incentive systems should be opposite of what most of them are. Costs should be fully acknowledged, reported, and treated right, not disguised, hidden, shifted to others, or masqueraded in reporting. All distortion is, finally, disabling.

25

The Marketing Mode

MARKETING IS, most importantly, a comprehensive view of the business process, a way of doing business that this view entails.

A business is an organized system of activities whose existence and level of success are based entirely on its ability to attract and hold a necessary number of solvent customers in some economically effective way. What a business does must be economically effective both for itself and its customers. In any case, customers usually have choices, not only as to whom to patronize and when, but also whether to buy at all. If they stop or reduce their buying, and especially from you, the business slows or stops.

The success of a business is centrally a function of how effectively attentive it is to the needs and wants of the people it tries to attract to its offerings, as well as the alternatives available to them. This does not mean that other things that companies do are less important, only that marketing is uniquely important. If enough people don't want to be your customer, if they don't stay being your customer, or don't like your prices even though they may like you and what you offer, or if they become dissatisfied with you for any reason—if any of these happen, the business is headed for trouble.

In a competitive world, getting and keeping customers requires innovation. Because somebody will always try to serve people better in order to merit their custom, you have to try better yourself. That requires innovating attitudes in all things—making products better, more suitable, more versatile, more easily operable and reparable; manufacturing them better and cheaper; improving dealings with customers and suppliers; improving effectiveness in the office, the sales force, the distribution system, and the trade. The marketing view of the business process requires that all innovation be thought of as intended to help get and keep customers, in short, to make the firm more competitive.

Though innovation is a necessity of business life, it is unnatural. It requires abandoning what's familiar and has been mastered for the unfamiliar and untried. Understandably, innovation does not happen automatically or easily. The only thing that's automatic is inertia—remaining with the accustomed and the comfortable.

Innovation has to be nurtured. If it is not specifically nurtured, its occurrence is likely to be merely accidental. It has to be made to happen. If it doesn't, the company declines. It declines because competitors (existing ones, start-up new ones) will surely find innovative new ways to serve customers better. There are usually lots of them, and they have the incentive to try.

One thing that is importantly new about our world is the intensified globalization of competition. Everybody is everywhere vulnerable to everybody else's commercial intrusions. There are not any longer any isolated or protected markets, no matter how small, remote, or specialized. Instant communication and cheap transport extend competitive reach, and in any case can aggregate small niche markets into scale-efficient global magnitudes. Nobody is exempt from the new competitiveness. Everybody has to manage better and seek innovations more systematically.

Innovation must constantly look for possibilities of product differentiation. In the pursuit of customers, every seller seeks to be in some appealing way different from all other sellers. Optimally, every seller tries to be irresistibly different. The aim is to become so distinctively different as to be, in effect, a monopolist of the offering—to be perceived as being not just the best provider of the particular product, but as being its *only* provider. Ideally, everybody else should be seen as being in a different and lesser league.

In this sense a product is not just the simple generic entity that we usually define it to be—such as, for example, cement, a disk drive, an evening dress, a particular software, lease financing, ship repair, a rock concert, satellite data services, or whatever. A product is not just its defined or descriptive core, but everything that is done with respect to it, including how it is packaged, sold, distributed, delivered, promoted, installed, repaired, field-supported and upgraded, how users are trained in its use, and much more.

A product is a complex cluster of value satisfactions. If the cluster is not sufficient and right, though its generic core (such as the disk or the cement) may be superb, if it is not "right" according to the wants and wishes of customers and compared to what is available from others, then it will not sell, or not sell well.

Differentiation is one of the most important strategic and tactical activities in which companies must constantly engage. It is not discretionary. And *everything* can be differentiated, even so-called "commodities" such as cement, copper, wheat, money, air cargo, marine insurance.

There is no such thing as a commodity, only people who act and think like commodities. Everything can be differentiated, as just observed, and usually is. Think only of soap, beer, investment banking, credit cards, steel warehousing, temporary help services, education. There is no reason for any company to get stuck in the commodity trap, forever confined to competing totally on price alone. Historically, companies that have taken and stayed resolutely on the commodity path, even when they have driven their costs deeply down, have become extinct.

Although the world is increasingly driven by high technology, it continues to be influenced and managed by high spirits—by emotion, energy, drive, persistence, and relationships that develop slowly over time between companies and individuals. Ironically, the more high-tech the world gets, the more important relationship management becomes for creating and keeping competitive advantage. This is a much misunderstood and neglected subject, especially among those trained in the physical sciences, engineering, and management science.

Nothing sells itself, not even, as we know so well, money or sex. When things must be sold, especially sold face-to-face, as is the case with the complex new products that appear with intensified frequency, much depends on the quality of the relationship between the seller and his intended customer. Relationships can be managed. To neglect them is to mismanage them.

Also much neglected is cultivation of the marketing imagination—the ability to make insightful leaps into the minds, emotions, and practices of customers, and into the vulnerabilities of competitors; leaps that help you to get and keep more customers. The marketing imagination is not terribly unique or elusive. It is not a talent, but a skill. It can be developed, cultivated, and enhanced. The problem is the false presumption that "you either have it or you don't."

Some of the biggest opportunities for the cultivation and exercise of the marketing imagination, and therefore for the practice of product differentiation, exist in intangible products—what are usually but not very helpfully called "services." Intangible products have certain unique properties. They can usually be more easily and quickly redesigned and less expensively customized and remanufactured than can processed or manufactured tangible products. Think only of how much insurance programs are customized and modified to suit particular people and situations, and similarly investment or commercial banking, industrial cleaning, travel, entertainment, legal services.

Possibilities for relatively easy and quick product customization and modification leave a lot of room for imaginative differentiation to the wants and wishes of individuals, segments, and markets, and to possibilities suggested by differences in time of day, day of week, and season. Such products lend themselves uniquely to the management of demand—as when airlines have special off-season or off-peak rates, hotels target particular groups for particular times with a wide mix of flexible offerings, preferred prospects get various preference treatments, restaurants offer early-bird and retiree discounts.

What is distinctive about all these examples is that the products are time-sensitive and perishable. When an airplane seat or a hotel room is empty, it remains forever unsold. You can try again another day, but never recover the lost day. That is the special incentive that drives the marketing imagination in these businesses, that inspires so much demand-producing innovation and differentiation—and still more possibilities exist, for these and for other industries.

Intangible product industries also lend themselves to the enhancing disciplines of industrial rationality and technology-based systems. Think only of the organizing rationality and the technological content of some familiar cases—of self-service retailers, cafeterias, fast-food chains, credit cards, credit clearing, mail and package services, warehousing and distribution, telephone and computerized brokerage, or reservations systems, and of the scheduled scrupulosity of preventive maintenance for machine tools, airplane engines, power stations, telecommunications systems, oil and chemical plants, bottling and canning lines, newspaper printing machines, and other "sensitive" facilities whose continuing and dependable workability most of us take for granted.

These examples show how much is regularly done to put technology, industrial routines, and organized rationality to work in intangible-product industries, and to provide the reliable and high-quality services that are so regularly bundled along with tangible products. More is surely possible if more attention is paid to the possibilities.

Intangible products, which you can't touch, see, smell, fondle, or easily test before buying them, also uniquely lend themselves to the reassuring possibilities of tangibilization, using visual or mnemonic devices to give substance to their promises. Examples are All-State Insurance, portraying itself visually as putting people into "safe hands"; Travelers Insurance, putting them securely under a conspicuously red umbrella; Prudential, suggesting itself visually as being "solid as the Rock of Gibraltar"; banks, projecting substantiality via architecture; law firms, suggesting prudentiality with conservative furniture and settings; hotels, suggesting hygienic cleanliness with bathroom drinking glasses wrapped in clinging plastic film and toilet seats sealed with fresh paper bands; repair and maintenance organizations, suggesting care and reliable professionalism by dressing their workers in fresh clean uniforms and having them conspicuously equipped with specialty tools and portable diagnostic devices strapped to their waists.

Everybody in every organization can develop a better marketing imagination and become better at practicing the marketing mode—the mode that helps companies (and even countries) to get better at getting and keeping customers. Everybody must. Because if you don't market, something terrible happens—nothing.

26

Trust in Advertising

ADVERTISING WORKS. It is not necessary to know exactly how it works in order to get it to work for you, though it helps to know approximately how it works—what makes it work, how it functions inside people's minds, and the like.

Whether people like, dislike, or are indifferent to advertising is irrelevant to whether it works, even on themselves. You do not admit that you bought something "because of the advertising," or that your choice was "influenced" by advertising. If you do, you usually refer to having bought a competing brand because the others' ads were so bad. It hardly matters. What matters is that it works, however mysteriously or perversely, however slowly or rapidly. It may not work as well as word of mouth, but it has the advantages of greater reach and being able to be targeted and controlled by the advertiser.

Every business should advertise, and every business does. Some do it more obviously than others. Some do it quietly and self-effacingly, precisely because that is how they think they'll be most effective with their intended audiences. The surgeon may choose not to run a display ad in the newspaper but will nevertheless have a listing in the yellow pages, and perhaps even in a special yellow-page listing of specializations. It should not be supposed that these are only for the convenience of forgetful colleagues or for the sake of a mother's pride.

The architect makes so-called "educational" presentations at seminars for developers and real-estate bankers. Lawyers put offices in the right sections of town and in the right buildings, belong to the right civic and social clubs and trade associations, and decorate their outer offices in what is presumed to suggest a suitable prudentiality. And for all, much care attends the selection of appropriate stationery, letterhead, and typeface. All is advertising, of course. It is communication designed to influence solvent prospects and present clients.

That is as it should be, not because of some absolute standard carved in the primeval rocks, but because everybody knows that people make decisions about you on the basis of the signals you emit. So it's best to be conscious of what you're doing, to try to give off the right and appropriate signals. That, in any case, is what people regularly do in deciding what clothes to wear for given occasions, what to say, how to behave. All is conscious presentation of oneself, and always it has a special purpose—to influence people into an intended direction.

"What's in a name?" Widely, this is viewed not as a question but as the voice of the cynic. "A rose/By any other name would smell as sweet." This is widely viewed as the voice of the versifier.

Why disagree? Because a name makes a difference, and it always did. "Who steals my purse steals trash; . . . /But he that filches from me my good name/ . . . makes me poor indeed." Shakespeare's character would have killed for the offense. The children's ditty goes, "Sticks and stones may break my bones, but words will never hurt me." More sensibly, the Chinese say, "Sticks may *only* break my bones, but words can really shatter me."

It is both fitting and indicative that there are so many memorable sayings about referential words, names, and labels. They have meaning, and meaning has the power to reassure, engage, attract, repel, outrage, disgust, compare, and enlist people into action. That also helps explain the existence of advertising.

Very little of advertising's purpose is to educate, explain, describe, or announce. New products get "announced," as do special prices or fashions of familiar ones, or their availability in unfamiliar places, such as in the home, where they are offered through the want ads. Complex products for informed or willing-to-learn customers get explained and described. But advertising serves different purposes. Some advertising tries to induce more frequent and bigger purchases. Much advertising is to attract buyers rather than have them go to or stay with competitors. Mostly, advertising is designed to destabilize the market in favor of the advertiser.

Almost all buying involves risk for the buyer—will what is offered work as promised or expected? Will it last? Will it fit, look okay in broad daylight, be suitable, be compatible, be installed as promised, get done in time; is it reparable; is the surgeon always reliable, will he be there if I need him the next day; will the lawyer be working for me or mostly for herself; will the bank's advice be reliable and will it be there when I really need it; will the supplier come across for us in times of shortages, will its system always be up-to-date and its repair crews prompt, etc. etc.?

These questions are not just a matter of getting the best or even a reasonable deal for your money; they are about trying to be reasonably sure about a lot of things involved in purchasing and its consequences. Mostly, they are about whether you can believe in the promise, the reliability of the vendor's word. They are about trust.

Advertising is mostly about building trust—about being perceived as and becoming a reliable source. The irony and the problem are that the better you do the more vulnerable you are to being perceived as failing. The more you promise about yourself—whether explicitly in words or implicitly in the various ways you represent yourself, such as in your stationery, your office appearance and location, your delivery vehicles, the performance, consistence, and design of your product, your packaging, salespeople, and telephone manners, your responsiveness to inquiries or calls for help, and the like—the more you promise and the more reliably you regularly deliver on your promise, the more people are likely to believe you. The more they believe you the more they trust you, and thus the more they are likely to deal with you. The more they believe in you the higher the chances you'll disappoint them. The more they deal with you the higher the chances you'll disappoint them.

The familiar saying "Familiarity breeds contempt" is the opposite of the truth. Familiarity breeds. "Out of sight, out of mind" is closer to the truth than "Absence makes the heart grow fonder." A familiar brand, a known company (which, behaviorally, often means a reliable company) is more likely to be chosen than a strange, remote, or anonymous one. In heavily advertised consumer goods this is especially obvious. It accounts for the inability over the years of house brands, private label brands, and no-brand products to climb out of the cellar of their obscurity, even though their prices are less, often substantially less.

Many people are price-sensitive, but with limits. In the case of packaged coffee, they switch brands fairly often, but mostly they switch among the well-known brands and on account of price promotions or price-off coupons. They seldom switch to the unknown or lower-priced house brands. When they do, usually they soon will switch back. In blind taste tests they can't tell the difference. But in actual use, with the package label showing, somehow the familiar brand seems better, or perhaps it says better things about people as buyers, users, providers for family or guests.

Purchasing should be quite sensibly viewed as risk-reducing behavior. The bigger the risk, the greater the caution, whether what's at stake is money, suitability, functionality, reliability, physical or psychological well-being, social standing, or professional repute. Reassurance can be strengthened by advertising—by what is said, its frequency, how, and where. All are obviously important and should preferably reinforce each other. Sometimes they unintentionally contradict each other. The right message shouted at a shrill pitch changes the message and its meaning. The environment in which it appears makes a difference—whether in, say, the *Harvard Business Review* or

Soldier of Fortune. The credibility of the message is affected by the medium in which it appears, its style, and its source. And, all other things being equal, the message, its source, and the brand are greatly and favorably affected by the familiarity that media advertising and direct encounter produce.

But a good thing is not necessarily improved by its multiplication. By some standard, advertising can be too frequent, too familiar, and therefore become noisy, intrusive, aggravating. If we assume reasonable care as to tone, style, and frequency, familiarity boosts the brand and the company. The better and clearer the promise, the more reliable and credible the brand, product, or supplier are likely to seem. If we have engendered more trust, customer preference is more likely to ensue.

As previously noted, so is customer disappointment. Performance in deed or consumption rarely matches advance expectations, though the consumer is often forgiving—in products such as cosmetics, consumer expectations are usually lower than what the advertiser seems to promise. The fibs and exaggerations contained in the metaphors and similes commonly employed in cosmetics and beauty-aid advertising are generally treated as benign, inoffensive, permissible, and even welcome. They provide satisfying fantasies of possibilities known to be only fantasies.

But for most products, the irony of using advertising (and other communications) to build familiarity and trust is that it also heightens customer expectations. The more appealing and persuasive the promise, the greater the likelihood of customer disappointment. Such sellers are more vulnerable to seeming to the customer to have under-fulfilled their promise. Once some degree of trust is estab-

143

lished, it becomes the basis for fixing blame on the one on whom it was bestowed. When something doesn't go quite right, there come comments such as, "I might have expected something like that from some obscure brand, but not from this one. How disappointing." Or, "Well, I couldn't help it, I bought the best. What can you do?" These are the sounds of backlash, grist for word-of-mouth badmouthing. The violation of trust has conveniently absolved the violated from responsibility for their own disappointment, and given them permission to fight back. It follows that the better the reputation the more carefully it has to be curried.

Advertising works because the familiar is safer than the unfamiliar. Those who make themselves visible and thereby familiar imply by their regular, good-sounding open advertisements that they'll always be around to "stand behind" the product, that it will be reliably right and safe, will stay up-to-date, and is fairly priced. The promises say that such sellers have confidence in their products and in everybody who directly represents them, and that they don't hesitate to make these promises for fear of embarrassment or consumer backlash if there is underperformance. These sellers are so sure of their product and their representatives that you can be sure too.

For reasons that may be mysterious but seem everywhere to prevail, you, the buyer, believe that your friends, neighbors, family, and colleagues will think well of you for dealing with the more familiar or well-thought-of brand or vendor. It matters not why this is so, only that in all societies (even, indeed, in the animal kingdom), it has always been so. Strangers are avoided if not actually suspected or attacked, the familiar tolerated if not necessarily welcomed or embraced, the known always preferred to the unknown.

Familiarity breeds. Contrary presumptions notwithstanding, this is especially more so in business-to-business affairs than in consumer goods and services. More things are so where they are generally believed not to be so than where they are commonly held to be so.

27

The Law of the Lunch

THE GENERAL RULE may be laid down that in all of human-kind's institutions, especially in business, government, and the priestly employments, there is an inverse relationship between how much their literatures and instructions attend to a particular activity and the actual importance of that activity. The greater the attendance, the less important it is; the less the attendance, the more important.

By that principle, few things in business are as important as the business lunch, about which absolutely nothing can be found in textbooks, casebooks, MBA programs, seminars, or conferences.

The business lunch is a pervasive institution, virtually obligatory, and everywhere conducted according to a fixed ritual. He who invites pays. Conversation starts and for long remains in the realm of seemingly idle chatter about personal interests in recreations, entertainments, family matters, and mutual acquaintances. Business is finally and gradually crept up on with careful avoidance of any implications that the lunch exists specifically to enhance the lunchee's opinions about the lunchor and the lunchor's assessment of the lunchee.

The business lunch and its rituals are based on the established fact that important buying decisions are rarely made on price alone, or alone on specifications, technical service, delivery, or vendor competence and reputation. The lunch exists to learn about things that are not said, to help establish and cement relationships of personal trust and understanding, to create commercial friendships and reciprocities, to facilitate favors hoped for and favors given, to go beyond technicalities and legalities in getting and cementing some sort of sale.

So don't knock it.

Index

Abandonment, 12–13
"Acres of Diamonds" (Conwell), 75
Action vs. talk, 43
Administration vs. management, 45–46
Advertising, 138–145
Africa, 90
Age, 58, 60–61
Agility, 94
Analysis, 43, 94
Arrogance, 30
Attitudes, 45
Authority, 43–44

Bad performance, 12–15
Bernoulli theorem, 45
Betterness, 51–54
Bureaucracy, 26
Business lunch, 146–147
Business-to-business transactions, 116–123

Capitalism, 75
Cash flow, 14
Change, 51–95
Charisma, 30
Chastity, 41

Childhood, 17, 22
Chryslerization of America, 99–102
Cities, decline of, 83, 86
Colleagues, 11, 13, 14
Command, 29–32
Competing on quality, 112–113
Competing on time, 113, 114
Competing through service, 112
Competing via information, 113
Competition, global, 101, 107, 133
Competitive advantage, 112, 134
Competitive analysis, 26, 112
Competitors, curiosity about, 52
Computer-networked home worker, 56, 87
Computers, 94
Computer software, 122
Con artist, 37, 122
Conscience, 38, 111
Consensus, 30
Consent, 30
Consumption, pluralization of, 103–108
Control, 26
Convictions, 30, 42–47, 95
Cost evasions, 124–130
Courage, 95
Credit cards, 122

Customers, 109–111, 136–137
advertising and, 138–145
attracting and holding, 113–115, 131–135
curiosity about, 52
market research and, 45

Daring, 14
Data, abundance of, 6
Decision-making, 25–28, 30–32, 95
change and, 45
staff and, 8–9
Decisiveness, 14, 25, 30, 31, 95
Demographics, 4
Design for manufacturability, 113
Desktop printing, 119
Discipline, 26, 27
Discrimination, in data supply and use, 6

Early retirement, 61, 102
Education, institutionalization of, 18
Energy, 23, 43, 44, 58
Entrepreneurship, 73–80, 113, 115
Environment, 92
Ethics, 39–41, 111
Ethnic food specialties, 105
Ethnicity, 104, 107
Ethnic separatism, 90

Excellence, 112
Experience, 7, 9–10, 18, 44, 58, 94
Experience curve, 112
External design appearances of products, 119

Fast history, 70–72, 82, 93–95
Fast response, 114
Finance, 109–111
Flattening the organization, 113
Flexible manufacturing, 112
Focused factory, 112
Forecasting, 46, 70
France, 73, 74
Full-absorption costing, 129, 130
Futurism, 81–95

Global competition, 101, 107, 133
Globalization, 90, 103–108
Good deeds, 37
Gorbachev, Mikhail, 83
Gradualism, 72
Greed, 33–38
Gross margins, 127–128
Gross profit, 128

Happenstance, 23
Hebraic and hellenic standards of judgment, 37
Heterogeneity, 104

Ideas, deeds and, 44
Immigration, 92
Inaction, 43
Incentives, negative, 5
Ineffectualness, 13
Inertia, 31, 46–47, 132
Information
    effective use of, 6
    metabolizing, 46
Inner self, 120
Innovation, 55–57, 64–66, 68, 113, 132–133
Insider trading, 33–34
Inspiration, 26, 27, 95
Insurance programs, 135, 137
Intangible-product industries, 135–137
Intelligence, 22, 23
International Monetary Fund, 92
Intrapreneurship, 74
Inventory, 5
IQ intelligence, 23
Irish Tourist Board, 7
Irresolution, 14

Joint-allocation costing, 125, 129
Judgment, 37
Junk bonds, 100

Kaizen, 51, 53
Knowledge
    management and, 16–19
    subconscious, 17

Knowledge workers, 18, 19, 22

Lay-offs, 14–15
Leadership, 29–30, 65
Likelihood, 56
Line/staff differences, 20–22
Listening, 43
Long-range planning, 26, 112
Lunch, 146–147

Management
    administration vs., 45–46
    knowledge and, 16–19
    mobility of professionals, 18–19
    training and selection, 18
    youthification of, 58–63
Management by objectives, 112
Management information system, 6
Managerial potential, 21–24, 31
Manager's career, 42
Market analysis, 26
Market fragmentation, 91
Marketing, 109–111, 113–115, 131–137
Marketing imagination, 135–137
Market research, 45
Market segments, 103, 105–107
Market share, 14, 115

Mass markets, 103, 104
Medical care, 92
Mediocrity, 14
Memorandum, 43
Microsegmentation, 91
Mitterand, François, 83
Mobility of professional managers, 18–19
Modernity, 107
Money, 34–37, 75, 109–111
Morality, 37–38, 40, 41, 111
Motion pictures, 122
Motive, 36–37
Murphy's law, 126
Musical recordings, 122

Names, 139–140
Nationalism, 90, 104, 107
Naziism, 84
Negative incentives, 5
Networked home computer, 56, 87
New product costs, 125–128
Newton's first law, 31
Not-good managers, 11–15

Office of the future, 56
Operating, 99–147
Order, 26, 120
Organization, 42
    innovating, 64–66
Overhead, 125, 129

Parochialism, 90, 104
Parsimony, 6

Performance, bad, 12–15
Personal qualities, 22, 23, 29
PIMS, 112
Planning, 112
Poland, 77–79
Polarization, 90
Portfolio strategy, 112
Potential, managerial,
   21–24, 31
Prescription, 26
Problem-solving, 90
Product differentiation,
   133–136
Productivity per employee,
   14
Product quality, 114
Psychology, 120
Purchasing decisions,
   116–123, 142

Quality, 114
Questions, 3–4

Rambo, 75
Rank, 43
Rascality, 39–41
Reagan White House, 39
Regionalism, 90
Religious dogmatism, 104
Religious factionalism, 90
Reputation, 122, 123
Research and development
   (R&D), 26, 57, 68, 83
Restructuring, 100, 101, 113,
   115

Retailing, 30
Retirement, 61, 102
Return on managed assets,
   14
Rhetoric, 43
Routine, 26, 30, 31, 57, 64,
   66

School performance, 23
Segments, market, 103,
   105–107
Selection of managers, 18
Self-doubt, 14
Self-examination, 66
Self-interest, 33–38
Self-managed teams, 113,
   115
Semiconductor electronics, 72
Service guarantees, 113
Services
   marketing imagination and,
     135–137
   quality and delivery of,
     114, 121, 122
Shrewdness, 95
Sin, 38
Small firms, 67–69
South Africa, 92
Soviet Union, 78, 79
Space age, 85
Specialized knowledge, 22,
   23
Spencerian principles, 14
Sputnik, 85
Stability, 69, 71, 94

Staff, decision-making and, 8–9

Staff/line differences, 20–22

Strategic intent, 113

Strategic planning, 112

Strategy, 112–114, 120

Subconscious knowledge, 17

Subordinates, effective, 43

Success, 51–54

Superbowl, 75

Swagger, 30

Takeovers, 92, 101

Teapot Dome scandal, 39

Technology, 5, 21, 72, 134

Television, 92

Theory, 7, 93

Thinking, 3–47

Tide, 53

Time, 59, 60

Timing, 23

Title, 44

Trade unions, 83

Training of managers, 18

Trends, 84

Trust, 121–123
    in advertising, 138–145

Virtue, 40

Vision, 26, 27, 94

Warfare, 21

Watergate, 39

Watson, Thomas, 118

Welfare, 92

Will to act, 95

Wisdom, 58, 94

World Health Organization, 92

Youthification of manage-ment, 58–63